Usborne
First
Illustrated
MATH
Dictionary

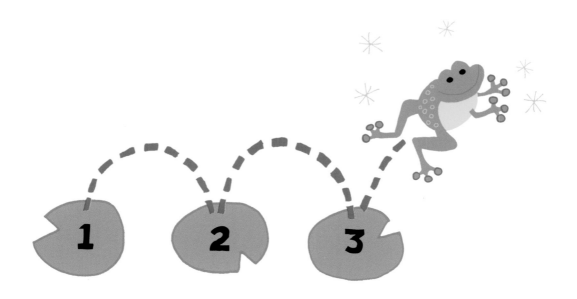

Usborne Quicklinks

There are some really good websites where children can watch animated explanations and practice their math skills with puzzles and games. We have selected the best sites and provided links to them from the Usborne Quicklinks website.

To visit the recommended websites, go to Usborne Quicklinks at www.usborne.com/quicklinks and enter the keywords: first math

Internet safety

We recommend that young children are supervised while on the internet and that they follow the internet safety guidelines displayed on the Usborne Quicklinks website. You'll find more tips and advice on staying safe on the internet there too.

The websites recommended in Usborne Quicklinks are regularly reviewed. However, the content of a website may change at any time and Usborne Publishing is not responsible for the content of websites other than its own.

Usborne
First Illustrated MATH Dictionary

Kirsteen Rogers

Designed and illustrated
by Karen Tomlins

Math education consultant:
Sheila Ebbutt BA, PGCE

What is math?

Math is short for mathematics. It's all about numbers, quantities and shapes. This book divides math into five different areas.

You can read straight through a section to find out all about a subject. Or use the word finder at the back of the book to look up particular words or topics.

Understanding numbers

This section tells you what numbers are and how they work. You will find numbers up to 1,000, as well as simple fractions.

Using numbers

In this section you'll find out about adding, subtracting, multiplying and dividing numbers.

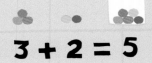

$$3 + 2 = 5$$

Understanding shapes and space

Here you can find out about different shapes and solids, and how you can change and move them in different ways.

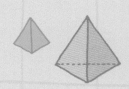

Measuring

This section will help you talk about and measure how long, wide, tall and heavy things are, and how much containers hold. There are useful sections about time and money, too.

Data

Data is information. This section shows you how to collect and understand information, and use graphs and charts to share it with other people.

Contents

Talking about amounts

An amount is "how many" or "how much" of something there is. Amounts include numbers and measurements. Here are some words you use to talk about amounts.

Some

Some means an amount of something. It does not tell you exactly how much, how many or how big the amount is.

some pizza   some pizza

A number of

A number of means there are separate things that you can count. It does not tell you exactly how many.

a number of candies   a number of lollipops

None

None means no amount.

Lots

Lots is a large number of things or a large amount of something.

lots of bees   lots of honey

Many

Many means a large number of things.

many stars

Few

Few means a small number of things.

a few cars

Numbers

There are so many numbers it is impossible to think of them all – in fact, they go on forever.

What do numbers do?

Numbers tell you "how many." Each number tells you about a different amount.

3 and 4 show different amounts.

You can use numbers as labels, to show which thing is which.

The numbers on these boats help people tell them apart.

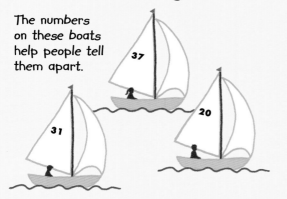

Numbers can be used as codes, such as in telephone numbers.

The numbers on a barcode are coded information, such as what the thing is and who made it.

ISBN 978-0-7945-3197-3

9 780794 531973 >

Staying the same

The number of things stays the same, no matter how you arrange them.

Here are 4 green marbles and 4 orange marbles.

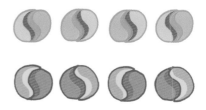

When you spread the green marbles out and count them, there are still 4.

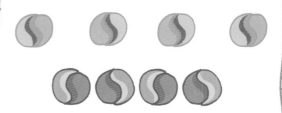

When you mix up all the marbles, there are still 4 of each color. What 4 means does not change.

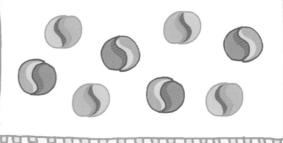

Zero

Zero is the number that stands for no amount. It is sometimes called nil or nothing.

This symbol means zero.

The number at the end of each row of buttons shows you how many buttons are in the row.

0

 **1**

Zero to ten

These pictures of buttons show how many each number from zero to ten stands for.

 2

You will sometimes see some numbers written in different styles, but they still mean the same.

Here are two styles of 1, 3, 4, 7 and 9.

 3

1 3 4 7 9
1 3 4 7 9

 **4**

More than ten

There are lots of numbers that are bigger than ten. They stand for bigger amounts.

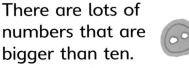 **5**

 6

7

 8

9

10

Number names

Each number has its own name. You write number names in words, like this.

two

six

You can see the number names from one to ten on page 14.

Digits

Digits are these ten symbols:

0123456789

Figures

When you write a number in figures, you use digits, like this.

2

6

Numerals

A numeral is a symbol or group of symbols that shows a number. Words and figures are numerals.

five word   **5** figure

Here are some more types of numerals showing five.

pictures

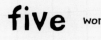

domino   dice

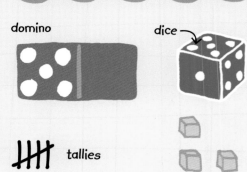

‖‖‖ tallies

V Roman numeral   blocks

六 Chinese numeral

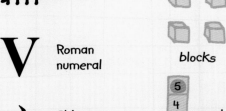

| 5 |
| 4 | number rod
| 3 |
| 2 |
| 1 |

number track

| 1 | 2 | 3 | 4 | 5 | 6 | 7 | 8 | 9 | 10 |

number line

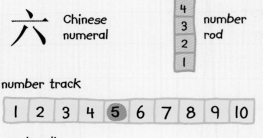

0 1 2 3 4 5 6 7 8 9 10

Find out more about: number lines and number tracks (page 24); tallies (page 13)

Zero to ten

Here are some different ways to show the numbers zero to ten.

0

zero, nil or nothing

Zero means nothing, so there is often nothing to see for zero.

1

one

2

two

3

three

4

four

5

five

6 six 卌 I

7 seven 卌 II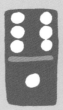

8 eight 卌 III

9 nine 卌 IIII

10 ten 卌 卌

Counting

People count things to find out how many there are. Here are some tips to help you count.

Using number names

As you count each thing, say or think the number names in order. The number you say when you count the last thing tells you how many there are.

To count these apples, say the numbers like this, starting with one:

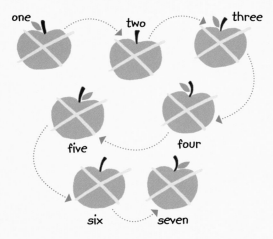

If it helps, touch or cross out each thing as you count it.

It does not matter what order you count the objects in. You can start and end on any object. But you must always say the numbers in the right order (one, two, three, four...).

Moving objects

When you count things that you can pick up, move each thing as you count it. This helps you remember which ones you have counted.

Here are some counters. You can move each counter to the side as you count it.

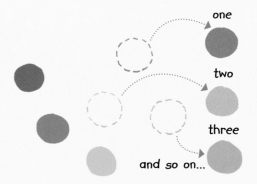

Or you can arrange them in one or more lines and count along the lines, touching each thing as you count it.

To count things that are moving, look at each group. 2 bees are sitting on the flower and now more are on their way... 3, 4, 5...

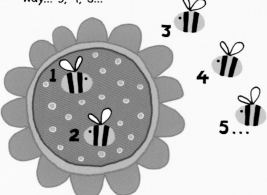

Using your fingers

You can use your fingers to help you keep track as you count things. Hold up one finger (or a thumb) for each thing you count.

When you count to 6, you will hold up 6 fingers.

Counting with your fingers is a good way to help you count things you can't always see but need to keep track of.

You could use your fingers to count how many butterflies visit a flowerbed while you watch.

Using tallies

You can use marks called tallies to keep track as you count things.

1. For each thing you count, draw a line like this:

2. As you say "five," draw a line across the others, like this.

3. When you have finished, count the tallies to find out how many things there are.

You could ask your friends if they like raspberry, strawberry or orange popsicles best, and use tallies to help you keep count.

Popsicles

Raspberry ||||| ||

Orange |||||

Strawberry ||||| ||||

These tallies show that 7 out of 20 people liked raspberry popsicles best. 4 people preferred orange ones. 9 people liked strawberry popsicles best.

13

1 one

2 two

Counting forward

As you count forward, each number you say is worth more than the last. Counting forward is another way of saying counting, or counting up.

3 three

Here are the numbers from one to ten. Each row has one more thing in it than the row above.

4 four

5 five

6 six

7 seven

8 eight

9 nine

10 ten

10 ten

9 nine

8 eight

7 seven

6 six

5 five

4 four

Here are the numbers from ten to one. Each row has one thing fewer in it than the row above.

3 three

Counting down

As you count down, each number you say is worth less than the last. Counting backward is another way of saying counting down.

2 two

1 one

Number names from zero to one hundred

To count things, you need to know the number names, the order they come in, and what each number means.

Here are the numbers zero to one hundred, in figures and words.

0	zero
1	one
2	two
3	three
4	four
5	five
6	six
7	seven
8	eight
9	nine
10	ten
11	eleven
12	twelve
13	thirteen
14	fourteen
15	fifteen
16	sixteen
17	seventeen
18	eighteen
19	nineteen
20	twenty

21	twenty-one
22	twenty-two
23	twenty-three
24	twenty-four
25	twenty-five
26	twenty-six
27	twenty-seven
28	twenty-eight
29	twenty-nine
30	thirty
31	thirty-one
32	thirty-two
33	thirty-three
34	thirty-four
35	thirty-five
36	thirty-six
37	thirty-seven
38	thirty-eight
39	thirty-nine
40	forty
41	forty-one
42	forty-two
43	forty-three
44	forty-four
45	forty-five
46	forty-six
47	forty-seven
48	forty-eight
49	forty-nine
50	fifty

51	fifty-one
52	fifty-two
53	fifty-three
54	fifty-four
55	fifty-five
56	fifty-six
57	fifty-seven
58	fifty-eight
59	fifty-nine
60	sixty
61	sixty-one
62	sixty-two
63	sixty-three
64	sixty-four
65	sixty-five
66	sixty-six
67	sixty-seven
68	sixty-eight
69	sixty-nine
70	seventy
71	seventy-one
72	seventy-two
73	seventy-three
74	seventy-four
75	seventy-five
76	seventy-six
77	seventy-seven
78	seventy-eight
79	seventy-nine
80	eighty

81	eighty-one
82	eighty-two
83	eighty-three
84	eighty-four
85	eighty-five
86	eighty-six
87	eighty-seven
88	eighty-eight
89	eighty-nine
90	ninety
91	ninety-one
92	ninety-two
93	ninety-three
94	ninety-four
95	ninety-five
96	ninety-six
97	ninety-seven
98	ninety-eight
99	ninety-nine
100	one hundred

Counting tip

Read down the list, saying each number as you go. Practice 0 to 10, then 0 to 20, and so on. Then try it without looking.

To count backward, read numbers upward, from the bottom of the list.

Counting to one hundred

Here are 100 birds. You can count 50 of them on this page...

...and 50 more on this page.

51   52   53   54   55

56   57   58   59   60

61   62   63   64   65

66   67   68   69   70

71   72   73   74   75

76   77   78   79   80

81   82   83   84   85

86   87   88   89   90

91   92   93   94   95

96   97   98   99   100

Counting to one thousand

Here are 1,000 flowers.

Turn the page to find out how to count to one thousand.

Number names from one hundred to one thousand

After one hundred, start counting from one again, but each time say "one hundred and..." first. Follow this pattern again for the two hundreds, three hundreds and so on, up to one thousand.

Here is the pattern to follow:

100	one hundred
101	one hundred and one
102	one hundred and two
103	one hundred and three
104	one hundred and four
105	one hundred and five
106	one hundred and six
107	one hundred and seven
108	one hundred and eight
109	one hundred and nine
110	one hundred and ten
111	one hundred and eleven
112	one hundred and twelve
113	one hundred and thirteen
114	one hundred and fourteen
115	one hundred and fifteen
116	one hundred and sixteen
117	one hundred and seventeen
118	one hundred and eighteen
119	one hundred and nineteen
120	one hundred and twenty

121	one hundred and twenty-one
122	one hundred and twenty-two
123	one hundred and twenty-three
124	one hundred and twenty-four
125	one hundred and twenty-five
126	one hundred and twenty-six
127	one hundred and twenty-seven
128	one hundred and twenty-eight
129	one hundred and twenty-nine
130	one hundred and thirty
131	one hundred and thirty-one
132	one hundred and thirty-two
133	one hundred and thirty-three
134	one hundred and thirty-four
135	one hundred and thirty-five
136	one hundred and thirty-six
137	one hundred and thirty-seven
138	one hundred and thirty-eight
139	one hundred and thirty-nine
140	one hundred and forty
141	one hundred and forty-one
142	one hundred and forty-two
143	one hundred and forty-three
144	one hundred and forty-four
145	one hundred and forty-five
146	one hundred and forty-six
147	one hundred and forty-seven
148	one hundred and forty-eight
149	one hundred and forty-nine
150	one hundred and fifty

151	one hundred and fifty-one
152	one hundred and fifty-two
153	one hundred and fifty-three
154	one hundred and fifty-four
155	one hundred and fifty-five
156	one hundred and fifty-six
157	one hundred and fifty-seven
158	one hundred and fifty-eight
159	one hundred and fifty-nine
160	one hundred and sixty
161	one hundred and sixty-one
162	one hundred and sixty-two
163	one hundred and sixty-three
164	one hundred and sixty-four
165	one hundred and sixty-five
166	one hundred and sixty-six
167	one hundred and sixty-seven
168	one hundred and sixty-eight
169	one hundred and sixty-nine
170	one hundred and seventy
171	one hundred and seventy-one
172	one hundred and seventy-two
173	one hundred and seventy-three
174	one hundred and seventy-four
175	one hundred and seventy-five
176	one hundred and seventy-six
177	one hundred and seventy-seven
178	one hundred and seventy-eight
179	one hundred and seventy-nine
180	one hundred and eighty

181	one hundred and eighty-one
182	one hundred and eighty-two
183	one hundred and eighty-three
184	one hundred and eighty-four
185	one hundred and eighty-five
186	one hundred and eighty-six
187	one hundred and eighty-seven
188	one hundred and eighty-eight
189	one hundred and eighty-nine
190	one hundred and ninety
191	one hundred and ninety-one
192	one hundred and ninety-two
193	one hundred and ninety-three
194	one hundred and ninety-four
195	one hundred and ninety-five
196	one hundred and ninety-six
197	one hundred and ninety-seven
198	one hundred and ninety-eight
199	one hundred and ninety-nine
200	two hundred and so on...

After one thousand

The number after nine hundred and ninety-nine is one thousand. But numbers don't finish there. After one thousand the numbers go up one by one through lots more thousands, then millions...
...and billions...
...and they keep going forever.

Number tracks

A number track shows numbers in order. Each space has a number in it. The numbers start at 1 and go up in size order.

number tracks

1	2	3	4	5	6

| 1 | 2 | 3 | 4 | 5 | 6 |

Number lines

A number line is a picture of numbers in order. Marks on the line are spaced evenly and each one stands for a number. The numbers go up in size order.

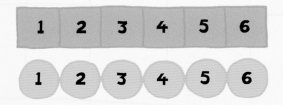

0   1   2   3   4   5   6

Lower numbers are at this side.

Higher numbers are at this side.

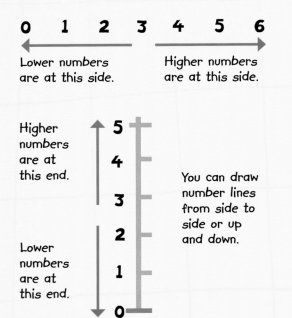

Higher numbers are at this end.

5
4
3
2
1
0

You can draw number lines from side to side or up and down.

Lower numbers are at this end.

A number line does not have to start at 0. It can start anywhere.

This number line starts at 13.

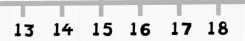

13 14 15 16 17 18

A number line does not need a number on every mark.

This number line starts at 0 and is numbered in fives. (Every fifth mark has a number.)

0   5   10   15

A number line does not need a mark for every number.

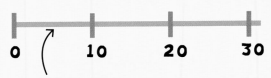

0   10   20   30

This part of the line stands for all the numbers between 0 and 10.

You can show fractions on number lines.

This number line shows some fractions between 0 and 1.

0          $\frac{1}{4}$ $\frac{1}{2}$ $\frac{3}{4}$ 1

Using number lines

You can use number lines, to show what you are doing when you count.

As you count you can move your finger or a pencil from one number to another. A move to the next number is called a step, hop or jump.

As you step, hop or jump to the right along a number line, the numbers get bigger.

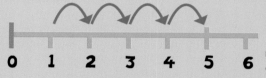

0 1 2 3 4 5 6

As you step, hop or jump to the left along a number line, the numbers get smaller.

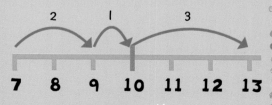

5 6 7 8 9 10 11

You can move along a number line with hops, steps or jumps of any size.

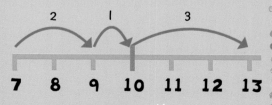

7 8 9 10 11 12 13

You could imagine a frog jumping along a number line.

You can use a number line to see or show how numbers are related to each other.

On this number line you can see that three jumps of one are the same as one jump of three.

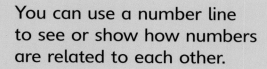
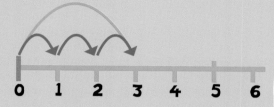

0 1 2 3 4 5 6

You can see that one jump of six is the same as two jumps of three, three jumps of two, and six jumps of one.

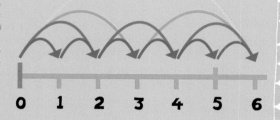

0 1 2 3 4 5 6

You can use number lines to show adding and subtracting.

26 and 2 more is 28.

24 25 26 27 28 29 30

42 take away 3 is 39.

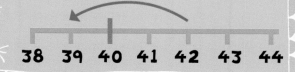

38 39 40 41 42 43 44

Find out more about: adding and subtracting (pages 56-74); left (page 102); right (page 102)

25

Counting forward

When you count forward, each number you say is bigger than the last one. You can start on any number to count forward.

There are 5 presents in the pile, and 1 more on its own is 6. There are 6 presents altogether.

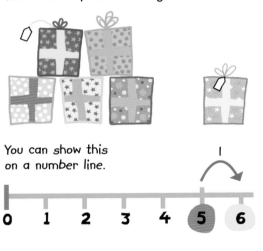

You can show this on a number line.

0 1 2 3 4 5 6

There are 9 arrows in the target, and 1 more that missed it. There are 10 arrows altogether.

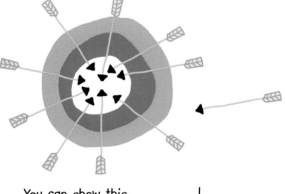

You can show this on a number line.

5 6 7 8 9 10 11

There are 2 pencils here, and 10 more in the package is 12. There are 12 pencils altogether.

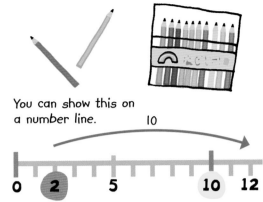

You can show this on a number line.

10

0 2 5 10 12

When you count up from a number, you start on that number and count forward.

When you count forward 2 from 9, you start on 9 and you land on 11.

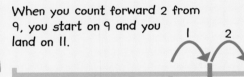

5 6 7 8 9 10 11

When you count up to a number, you keep counting until you reach that number.

When you start at 17 and count up to 20, you take 3 steps.

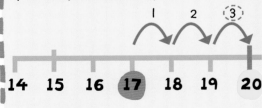

14 15 16 17 18 19 20

Counting forward is adding. You can read more about adding on pages 56 to 58, and 62 to 74.

Counting backward

When you count backward, each number is smaller than the last one. You can start on any number to count backward.

5 little birds are eating seeds.

One of the birds flies away.

Now there are 4 birds.

You can show this on a number line.

Lucky Ben has 10 chocolates.

He eats one.

Now he has 9. He has one fewer.

You can show this on a number line.

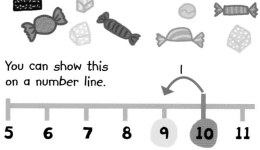

Find out more about: steps (page 25)

There are 13 bubbles here. If 10 of them burst, how many will be left?

You can show this on a number line.

There will be 3 bubbles left.

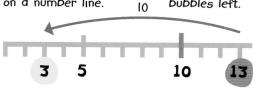

When you count back from a number, you start on that number and count backward.

When you count back 2 from 6, you land on 4.

When you count back to a number, you keep counting until you reach that number.

When you start at 12 and count back to 9, you take 3 steps.

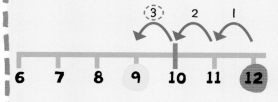

Counting back is subtracting. You can find out more about subtracting on pages 59 to 74.

Counting in twos, threes, fours, fives...

Instead of counting in hops, steps or jumps of one, you can count in twos, threes, or any other number. When you have a lot of things to count, counting like this is quicker than counting in ones. You are less likely to lose count too.

You can count these flowers two at a time.

You can show your counting on a number line.

On these number lines, the yellow circles show where you land with each jump when you start on the number in the pink circle.

When you count up in 2s, each number you say is two more than the last one. This number line shows what happens when you count in 2s from 0.

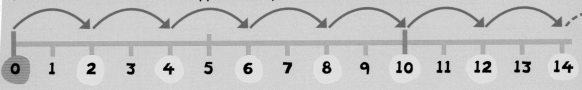

When you count in 3s, each number you say is three more than the last one. This number line shows what happens when you count in 3s from 21.

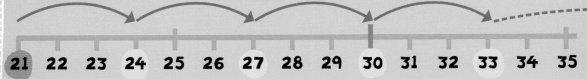

When you count in 4s, each number you say is four more than the last one. This number line shows what happens when you count in 4s from 12.

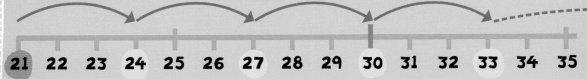

Remember, you don't have to write every number on a number line to show your counting.

When you count in 5s, each number you say is five more than the last one. This number line shows what happens when you count in 5s from 35.

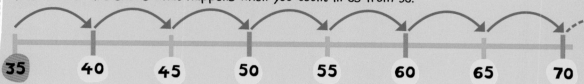

You can count back in twos, threes, or any other number too, and show your counting on a number line. Here are some examples.

When you count back in 2s, each number you say is two less than the last one. This number line shows what happens when you count back in 2s from 14.

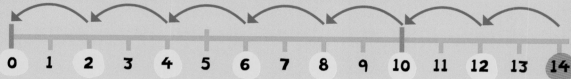

When you count back in 3s, each number you say is three less than the last one. This number line shows what happens when you count back in 3s from 29.

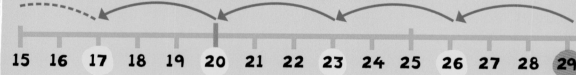

When you count back in 4s, each number you say is four less than the last one. This number line shows what happens when you count back in 4s from 40.

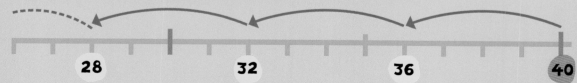

When you count back in 5s, each number you say is five less than the last one. This number line shows what happens when you count back in 5s from 63.

Counting in tens

You can count, and count forward and backward in tens. When you count forward in tens, each number you say is ten more than the last one. When you count backward in tens, each number you say is ten less than the last one. You can show your counting on a number line.

This number line shows what happens when you count on in 10s from 12.

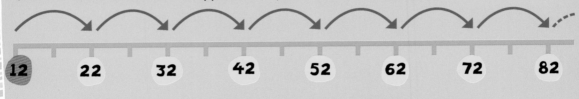

This number line shows what happens when you count backward in 10s from 99.

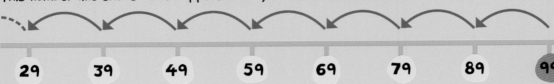

When you count in tens, the numbers follow a pattern.

All the numbers end in the same digit as the number you start from. When you count forward, the first digit is one more each time. When you count backward, it is one less each time.

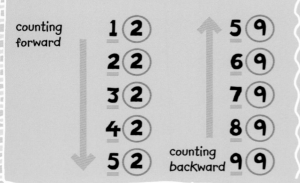

counting forward

1 **2**
2 **2**
3 **2**
4 **2**
5 **2**

5 **9**
6 **9**
7 **9**
8 **9**
counting backward 9 **9**

On this hundred grid you can see the pattern that numbers follow when you count forward and backward in tens.

counting forward from 12

1	2	3	4	5	6	7	8	9	10
11	12	13	14	15	16	17	18	19	20
21	22	23	24	25	26	27	28	29	30
31	32	33	34	35	36	37	38	39	40
41	42	43	44	45	46	47	48	49	50
51	52	53	54	55	56	57	58	59	60
61	62	63	64	65	66	67	68	69	70
71	72	73	74	75	76	77	78	79	80
81	82	83	84	85	86	87	88	89	90
91	92	93	94	95	96	97	98	99	100

counting backward from 99

Talking about numbers

You can describe numbers in lots of ways. On pages 31 to 35 you'll find some useful words to help you.

One-digit numbers

The numbers from zero to nine have one digit. They are called one-digit (or 1-digit) numbers.

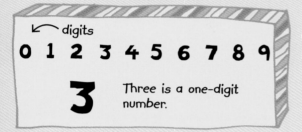

digits
0 1 2 3 4 5 6 7 8 9
3 Three is a one-digit number.

Two-digit numbers

You need two digits to write number ten in figures, so it is a two-digit (or 2-digit) number.

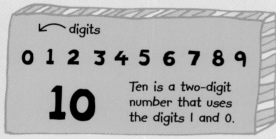

digits
0 1 2 3 4 5 6 7 8 9
10 Ten is a two-digit number that uses the digits 1 and 0.

All the whole numbers from ten to ninety-nine have two digits, so they are all two-digit numbers too.

some two-digit numbers

62 **21** **99**

Three-digit numbers

When you reach one hundred, you need three digits to write it down in figures. It is a three-digit (or 3-digit) number.

digits
0 1 2 3 4 5 6 7 8 9
100 One hundred is a three-digit number that uses the digits 1 and 0.

All the whole numbers from 100 to 999 have three digits, so they are all three-digit numbers too.

some three-digit numbers

221 **101**
538 **376**
999 **833**

Find out more about: whole numbers (page 54)

Four-digit numbers

When you reach one thousand, you need four digits to write it down in figures. It is a four-digit (or 4-digit) number.

← digits

0 1 2 3 4 5 6 7 8 9

1,000

One thousand is a four-digit number that uses the digits 1 and 0.

All the whole numbers from 1,000 to 9,999 have four digits, so they are all four-digit numbers too.

some four-digit numbers

1,001

2,236

1,237

9,999

8,750

It is not only how many digits a number has that makes it big or small, but also what the digits are worth. This is called place value, and you can find out more about it on pages 36 and 37.

Number grids

A number grid has squares with numbers on it. The numbers are in size order. Different number grids show different relationships between the numbers.

Here are some different number grids.

1	2	3
4	5	6
7	8	9

A nine grid shows groups of three.

1	2	3	4
5	6	7	8
9	10	11	12
13	14	15	16

A 16 grid shows groups of four.

1	2	3	4	5
6	7	8	9	10
11	12	13	14	15
16	17	18	19	20
21	22	23	24	25

A 25 grid shows groups of five.

Rows

In a row, numbers are next to each other, going across.

1	2	3
4	5	6
7	8	9

↖ row

Columns

In a column, numbers sit one above another, going up and down.

1	2	3
4	5	6
7	8	9

↖ column

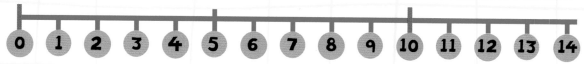

On this number line, the numbers on pink are even. The numbers on purple are odd.

Even numbers

All even numbers can be split up exactly into groups of two. 2, 4, 6, 8 and 10 are even numbers, and so are all numbers that have 2, 4, 6, 8 or 0 at the end.

2, 4, 6, 8 and 10 are even numbers.

The numbers on pink squares are even. They all end in 0, 2, 4, 6 or 8.

1	2	3	4	5
6	7	8	9	10
11	12	13	14	15
16	17	18	19	20
21	22	23	24	25

Odd numbers

Odd numbers can't be split up exactly into groups of two. There is always one left over. 1, 3, 5, 7 and 9 are odd numbers, and so are all numbers that have 1, 3, 5, 7 or 9 at the end.

1, 3, 5, 7 and 9 are odd numbers.

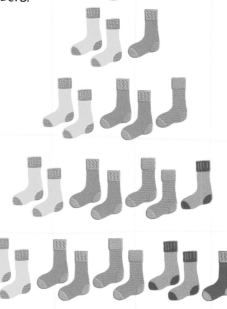

The numbers on purple squares are odd. They all end in 1, 3, 5, 7 or 9.

1	2	3	4	5
6	7	8	9	10
11	12	13	14	15
16	17	18	19	20
21	22	23	24	25

Find out more about: exactly (page 108); pairs (groups of two) (page 52)

"Tens" numbers

Two-digit numbers that end with 0 are "tens" numbers. After ten, their names end in "ty."

10	ten
20	twenty
30	thirty
40	forty
50	fifty
60	sixty
70	seventy
80	eighty
90	ninety

Teen numbers

The numbers eleven to nineteen are teen numbers. Most of their names end in "teen."

11	eleven
12	twelve
13	thirteen
14	fourteen
15	fifteen
16	sixteen
17	seventeen
18	eighteen
19	nineteen

Multiples

You can split a multiple of a number into groups of that number, with none left over.

You can split 9 into groups of 3, with none left, so 9 is a multiple of 3.

A number can be a multiple of more than one number.

You can split 10 into groups of 5, with none left, so 10 is a multiple of 5.

You can also split 10 into groups of 2, with none left, so 10 is a multiple of 2 as well.

The multiples of all numbers go on forever. These hundred grids show the multiples of 2, 3, 4, 5 and 10 up to 100.

When you show multiples of a number on a number grid, you can start to see patterns.

1	2	3	4	5	6	7	8	9	10
11	12	13	14	15	16	17	18	19	20
21	22	23	24	25	26	27	28	29	30
31	32	33	34	35	36	37	38	39	40
41	42	43	44	45	46	47	48	49	50
51	52	53	54	55	56	57	58	59	60
61	62	63	64	65	66	67	68	69	70
71	72	73	74	75	76	77	78	79	80
81	82	83	84	85	86	87	88	89	90
91	92	93	94	95	96	97	98	99	100

Multiples of 2 and 4 are all even numbers. They end in 2, 4, 6, 8 or 0.

1	2	3	4	5	6	7	8	9	10
11	12	13	14	15	16	17	18	19	20
21	22	23	24	25	26	27	28	29	30
31	32	33	34	35	36	37	38	39	40
41	42	43	44	45	46	47	48	49	50
51	52	53	54	55	56	57	58	59	60
61	62	63	64	65	66	67	68	69	70
71	72	73	74	75	76	77	78	79	80
81	82	83	84	85	86	87	88	89	90
91	92	93	94	95	96	97	98	99	100

Multiples of 3 can be odd or even.

1	2	3	4	5	6	7	8	9	10
11	12	13	14	15	16	17	18	19	20
21	22	23	24	25	26	27	28	29	30
31	32	33	34	35	36	37	38	39	40
41	42	43	44	45	46	47	48	49	50
51	52	53	54	55	56	57	58	59	60
61	62	63	64	65	66	67	68	69	70
71	72	73	74	75	76	77	78	79	80
81	82	83	84	85	86	87	88	89	90
91	92	93	94	95	96	97	98	99	100

Multiples of 5 all end in 5 or 0.

1	2	3	4	5	6	7	8	9	10
11	12	13	14	15	16	17	18	19	20
21	22	23	24	25	26	27	28	29	30
31	32	33	34	35	36	37	38	39	40
41	42	43	44	45	46	47	48	49	50
51	52	53	54	55	56	57	58	59	60
61	62	63	64	65	66	67	68	69	70
71	72	73	74	75	76	77	78	79	80
81	82	83	84	85	86	87	88	89	90
91	92	93	94	95	96	97	98	99	100

Multiples of 10 ("tens" numbers) end in 0.

1	2	3	4	5	6	7	8	9	10
11	12	13	14	15	16	17	18	19	20
21	22	23	24	25	26	27	28	29	30
31	32	33	34	35	36	37	38	39	40
41	42	43	44	45	46	47	48	49	50
51	52	53	54	55	56	57	58	59	60
61	62	63	64	65	66	67	68	69	70
71	72	73	74	75	76	77	78	79	80
81	82	83	84	85	86	87	88	89	90
91	92	93	94	95	96	97	98	99	100

Find out more about: number grids (page 32); even numbers (page 33); odd numbers (page 33)

Place value

All numbers are made up of digits. You need only 10 digits (0 to 9) to write any number you want. This is because of something called place value.

2   8
82   28
828   2,888
8,828   8,288

Here are some numbers you can write with the digits 2 and 8.

Place value

Each place in a number stands for a different amount.

This place stands for hundreds.

This place stands for tens.

This place stands for ones.

A digit's place value tells you how much the digit is worth in a number.

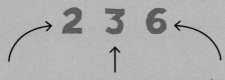

This 2 is worth 200.

This 3 is worth 30.

This 6 is worth 6.

Represents

Represents means "stands for."

Ones or units (O or U)

The ones place in a number stands for ones. Ones are sometimes called units.

Numbers that have only one digit show how many ones are in the number.

3 ● ● ●   3 stands for 3 ones.

In numbers with more than one digit, the ones place is always on the right.

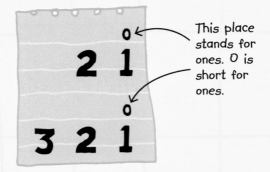

This place stands for ones. O is short for ones.

Groups and bundles

Tens and hundreds are groups of ones. A bundle is another word for a group.

one ● A ten is a group of ten ones.

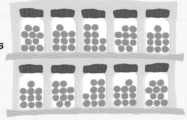

A hundred is a group of ten tens.

Tens (T)

The tens place in a number stands for groups of ten. It is to the left of the ones place.

This place stands for tens. T is short for tens.

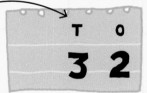

T O
3 2

Hundreds (H)

The hundreds place in a number stands for groups of one hundred. It is to the left of the tens place.

This place stands for hundreds. H is short for hundreds.

H T O
2 3 2

2-digit place value

The digits in 2-digit numbers show how many tens and ones there are.

23 is made up of 2 tens and 3 ones.

T O
2 3

You can use an abacus to see how place value works. The beads on this abacus show the number 23.

T O

3-digit place value

The digits in 3-digit numbers show how many hundreds, tens and ones.

147 is made up of 1 hundred, 4 tens and 7 ones.

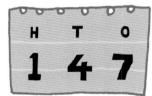

H T O
1 4 7

You can use base ten blocks to see how place value works.

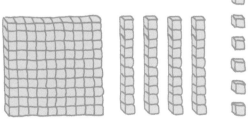

You can show 147 with 1 hundreds block, 4 tens blocks and 7 ones blocks.

Find out more about: left (page 102)

Bigger place values

The places at the beginning of numbers with 4 or more digits stand for other amounts, such as thousands, tens of thousands and so on.

thousands

Th   H   T   O
1, 0   0   0

The last three places are always hundreds, tens and ones.

So, 2,314 stands for 2 thousands, 3 hundreds, 1 ten and 4 ones.

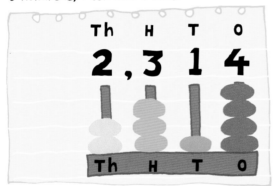

Th   H   T   O
2 , 3   1   4

The place value chart below shows the different place values of digits in numbers with 1, 2, 3 and 4 digits.

Zero as place holder

Zero (0) stands for no amount. A zero in a number is important because it holds a place. This stops the digits from making a different number.

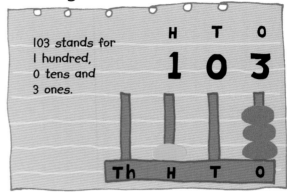

103 stands for 1 hundred, 0 tens and 3 ones.

H   T   O
1 0 3

Without the 0 holding the tens place, the 103 would only be 13.

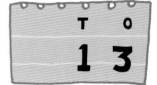

T   O
1 3

These tens blocks show that 103 and 13 are very different numbers.

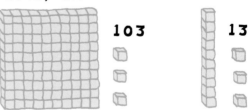

103

13

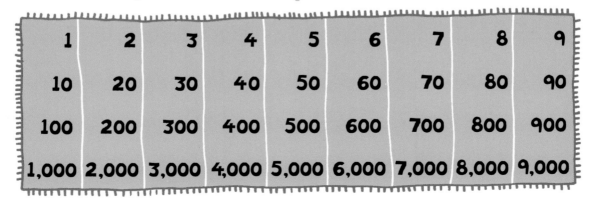

1	2	3	4	5	6	7	8	9
10	20	30	40	50	60	70	80	90
100	200	300	400	500	600	700	800	900
1,000	2,000	3,000	4,000	5,000	6,000	7,000	8,000	9,000

Partitioning

You can split numbers up into smaller numbers that have the same total value. This is called partitioning. You can use place value to partition numbers.

You can use place value to partition 28 into 20 (2 tens) and 8 (8 ones).

T	O
2	**8**

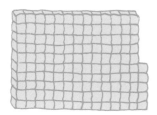 is the same as:

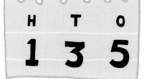 and

You can partition 135 into 100 (1 hundred), 30 (3 tens) and 5 (5 ones).

H	T	O
1	**3**	**5**

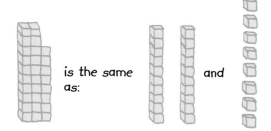

is the same as:

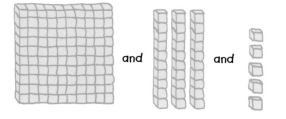

and   and

Exchanging

When you exchange something you trade it for something else. Sometimes in math it is useful to exchange one value for another one.

You can exchange ten ones for a group of ten.

You can also exchange a group of ten for ten ones.

You can exchange a hundred for ten groups of ten.

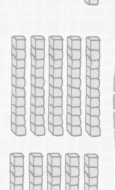

You can also exchange ten tens for one hundred.

Writing numbers

You can use the digits 0 to 9 to show any number you want. When you know the digits and "tens" numbers, place value can help you write numbers more than 20 in words and figures.

Writing 2-digit numbers

To write 2-digit numbers in words, write down the tens part first, then the ones part.

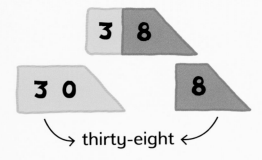

To write a 2-digit number in figures, write down the first digit of the "tens" number, and then the ones digit.

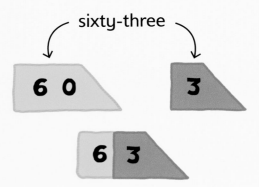

Writing 3-digit numbers

To write 3-digit numbers in words, write the hundreds first, then the tens, then the ones.

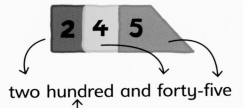

Write "hundred" not "hundreds."

To write a 3-digit number in figures, write the first digit of the hundreds, then the first digit of the tens, then the ones digit.

When there are no tens, write a 0 to hold the place.

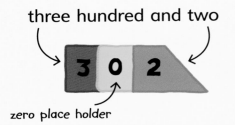

zero place holder

 Find out more about: 2-digit numbers, 3-digit numbers (page 31); digits (page 9); place value (pages 36-38); "tens" numbers (page 34)

Comparing numbers

People compare numbers to see if they are the same or different. Here are some words you can use to compare the size of numbers.

"Same" words

These words tell you that a number is just like, or is worth as much as, another one.

same . equivalent

as many as

equal

the same number as

= This symbol means "is equal to," "is the same as" and "is equivalent to."

There is the same number of blue butterflies as yellow butterflies.

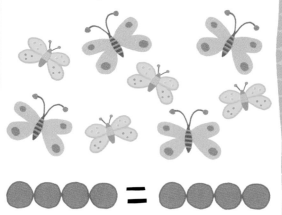

Exactly

A number that is exactly the same as another one is no bigger and no smaller.

The orange house has exactly the same number of windows as the purple house.

Almost

Almost means nearly.

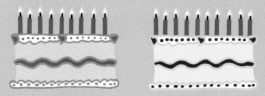

The pink cake has almost as many candles on it as the yellow one.

Different from

Things that are not the same as each other are different. Numbers can be different by being bigger or smaller.

"Bigger than" words

These words describe a number that is bigger than another one.

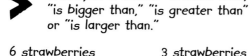

bigger · greater · more · larger

> This symbol means "is more than," "is bigger than," "is greater than" or "is larger than."

6 strawberries   3 strawberries

You can say that six is greater than, larger than, more than or bigger than three.

You can write: **6 > 3**

Numbers get bigger as you read this way along a number line. ⟶

| 0 | 20 | 40 | 60 | 80 | 100 |

27   73   89

89 is more than 73, which is bigger than 27.

More means a bigger number of things.

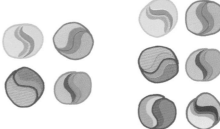

some marbles   more marbles

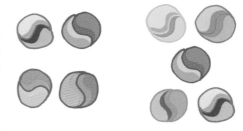

4 marbles   one more

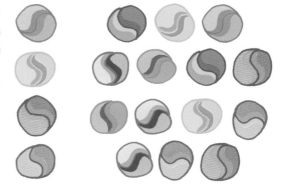

4 marbles   ten more

"Biggest" words

The greatest or largest number, or the most, is the biggest of three or more numbers.

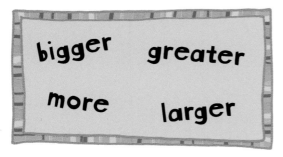   

some   more   the most

"Smaller than" words

These words describe a number that is smaller than another one.

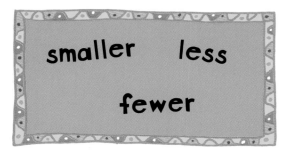

smaller   less

fewer

 This symbol means "is less than" or "is smaller than."

3 raspberries   5 raspberries

You can say that three is smaller than five or that three is less than five.

You can write: **3 < 5**

Numbers get smaller as you read this way along a number line.

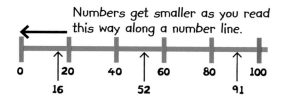

16 is smaller than 52, which is less than 91.

Fewer is another way of saying a smaller number of things. People often say "less" to mean fewer too.

some marbles   fewer marbles
(3 is less than 4.)

3 marbles   one fewer
(2 is less than 3.)

11 marbles   ten fewer
(1 is less than 11.)

"Smallest" words

The least number of, or the fewest, is the smallest of three or more numbers.

few   fewer   the fewest

43

Ordering

Things that are in order are in the right place. Numbers, letters and days of the week have an order.

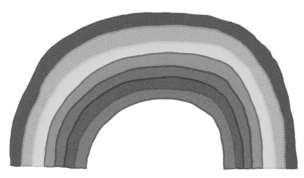

The colors in a rainbow are always in the same order.

Order of numbers

When you learn to count, you learn the numbers in order. (You can find out more about counting on pages 14 to 23.) Knowing the order of numbers can help you in lots of ways.

You will know
...that there are more balloons in this package than in this one.

↓   ↓

...that 6 o'clock is earlier in the morning than 8 o'clock...

...and that page 44 comes before page 45.

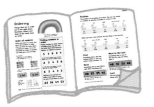

Putting numbers in order

Putting numbers in order means arranging them by size. You can order them from lowest to highest, or highest to lowest.

5   3   6   2   4

To order these numbers from lowest to highest, start with the smallest number.

2   3   4   5   6

To order them from highest to lowest, start with the biggest number.

6   5   4   3   2

Numbers do not have to follow each other in ones for you to put them in order.

22   36   49   53

Positions

The position of something is its place. You can use words or numbers to describe a position in a line or a list.

first	next	middle	next to the last	last
1st	2nd	3rd	4th	5th
first	second	third	fourth	fifth

When you turn a line around, the first thing is now the last.

last	next to the last	middle	next	first
5th	4th	3rd	2nd	1st
fifth	fourth	third	second	first

First

Something that is first has nothing before it. You can write it using numbers: 1st.

Next

Something that is next follows right after something else.

26 33 39 42

The first number in this list is 26. The next one is 33.

Next to the last

Something that is next to the last has only one thing after it.

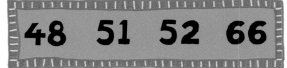

48 51 52 66

52 is the next to the last number in this list. The last number is 66.

Last

The last thing has no more things after it.

Find out more about: position (pages 99-101)

In this line of cars, the pink car is *before* the yellow car and *before* the purple car.

The red car is *after* the green car and after the purple car.

Before

Before means in front of. For example, May is before June and page 46 is before page 47. A number that is before another one is one you count earlier.

20 comes *before* 22 and 28.

After

After means behind. For example, Wednesday is after Tuesday, and page 18 is after page 15. When a number is after another one, you count the other number first.

36 comes *after* 28 and after 26.

Above

Above means higher up. It can describe a higher place, such as on a ladder or in a list. It can also mean a bigger amount: 35 is above 34.

28 inches is *above* 21 inches and below 35 inches.

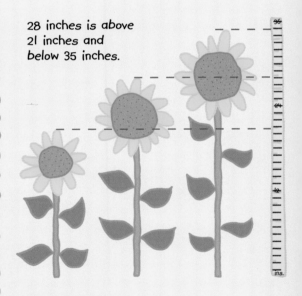

Below

Below means lower down. It can describe a lower place, such as on a ladder or in a list. It can also mean a smaller amount: 50 is below 52.

Between

Something that is between has things on either side of it, or above and below it.

The burger is between two pieces of bread.

5 6 7 8

The numbers between 5 and 8 are 6 and 7. They do not include 5 and 8.

Halfway between means there are exactly the same number of things on either side.

50   60   70

60 is halfway between 50 and 70. It has the same number of markers on either side.

Something that is halfway between is in the middle.

Ordinal numbers

Ordinal numbers tell you about order. Except for numbers that end in -first, -second, -third, all ordinal numbers end in "th."

You use ordinal numbers for dates.

Please come to my 6th Birthday Party on September 21st at 3 o'clock. From Charlie

1st	first	**11th**	eleventh	**21st**	twenty-first
2nd	second	**12th**	twelfth	**22nd**	twenty-second
3rd	third	**13th**	thirteenth	**23rd**	twenty-third
4th	fourth	**14th**	fourteenth	**24th**	twenty-fourth
5th	fifth	**15th**	fifteenth	**25th**	twenty-fifth
6th	sixth	**16th**	sixteenth	**26th**	twenty-sixth
7th	seventh	**17th**	seventeenth	**27th**	twenty-seventh
8th	eighth	**18th**	eighteenth	**28th**	twenty-eighth
9th	ninth	**19th**	nineteenth	**29th**	twenty-ninth
10th	tenth	**20th**	twentieth	**30th**	thirtieth

and so on...

Patterns and sequences

A sequence is a set of things that are in order and follow a particular rule. Pictures, shapes and numbers can follow sequences.

Relationships

A relationship describes the difference between one number in a sequence and the next.

20 21 22 23...

The relationship here is that each number is one more than the last.

35 33 31 29...

The relationship here is that each number is two less than the last.

Rules

A rule is a pattern that a sequence follows. There are lots of different rules.

20 21 22 23...

The rule here is "add 1."

35 33 31 29...

The rule here is "take away 2."

Every other

Every other thing means every second thing. Another word for every other is alternating.

Every other penguin has a blue hat, and every other penguin has a red hat.

Predict

You predict something when you say what you think will happen next. To predict missing parts of a sequence, find the rule then use it to fill in the spaces.

Continue

To continue a sequence you draw or write the pictures or numbers that come next.

48 Find out more about: adding (pages 56-58); even numbers (page 33); finding the difference (page 60); odd numbers (page 33); ordering (page 44); taking away, or subtracting (pages 59-61)

Picture sequences

A picture sequence is a list of pictures that follow a rule. Another name for a picture sequence is a picture pattern.

The next milkshake will have four straws.

The next drink will be pink, with a pink straw.

Number sequences

A number sequence, or number pattern, is a list of numbers that follow a rule.

20 23 26 29 ?

This number sequence follows the rule "add 3." The next number will be 32.

The sequences of odd and even numbers use the rule "add 2."

Odd numbers

1 3 5 7 9 11...

Even numbers

2 4 6 8 10 12...

Finding the rule

To find the rule in a sequence, find the difference between each pair of numbers or things and write them in the gaps.

When the numbers are getting bigger, the rule may be to add (imagine counting forward along a number line).

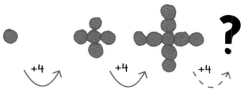

The rule here is "add 1 more to the end of each cross." The next cross will have 13 circles in it.

The rule is "add 5." Add 5 to the last number to continue the sequence (40).

When the numbers are getting smaller, the rule may be to take away (imagine counting backward along a number line).

The rule here is "take away 10." The next number in the sequence will be 50.

Rounding numbers

Rounding means giving a number another value that is close to it. People sometimes round numbers to make them easier to use or easier to remember.

Rounding up

Rounding up means giving a number a higher value.

These prices have been rounded up.

Rounding down

Rounding down is giving a number a lower value.

These prices have been rounded down.

The nearest 10

To round to the nearest 10, give a number the value of the "tens" number it is closest to. When the ones digit is 5 or more, round up. When it is 4 or less, round down.

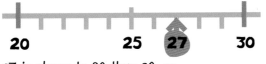

27 is closer to 30 than 20, so you round it up to 30.

24 is closer to 20 than 30, so you round it down to 20.

The nearest 100

To round to the nearest 100, give a number the value of the hundreds number it is closest to. When the tens digit is 5 or more, round up. If it is 4 or less, round down.

260 is closer to 300 than 200, so you round it up to 300.

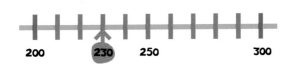

230 is closer to 200 than 300, so you round it down to 200.

Estimating numbers

Estimating means taking a good guess. Instead of counting everything, you can make an estimate of an amount.

There are about 15 ladybugs here.

Estimate

An estimate is a good guess.

You can estimate the position of a number on a number line.

4 would be a little less than halfway along this 0-10 number line.

To estimate how many things there are in a group, split the groups into smaller groups that are about the same size. Count how many things are in one group then multiply this number by the number of groups.

(Find out about multiplying on pages 75-77.)

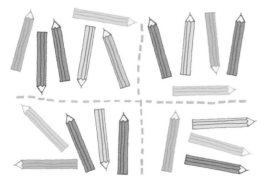

There are 4 groups with about 5 crayons in each group, so there are roughly 20 (4 sets of 5) crayons altogether.

Estimating words

All these words give clues that a number is an estimate.

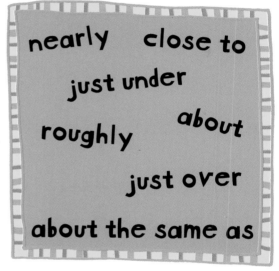

nearly   close to
just under
about
roughly
just over
about the same as

Comparing estimates

You can compare estimates of things to see if you have the number you need.

You can estimate the number of cookies and cherries to tell if there are enough cherries to put one on each cookie, or if there are too many, or too few.

Find out more about: comparing numbers (pages 41-43); comparing sizes (pages 106-107)

Groups

A group is two or more things that go together, or are like each other in some way.

Group names

Sometimes a group's name can tell you its size. Twos are groups of two. Tens are groups of ten, and so on. Some groups have special names as well.

Pairs

A pair is a group of two things.

a pair of shoes

Dozens

A dozen is a group of twelve things.

a dozen roses

Half dozens

A half dozen (or half a dozen) is a group of six things.

half a dozen eggs

Things you buy are often sold in groups.

a package of 5 suckers

a bunch of bananas

a set of 2 pairs of socks

```
|---|---|---|---|---|---|---|
0   5   10  15  20  25  30
```

This number line is marked in fives (groups of five).

Sets

A set is another name for a group. People sometimes call a group a set when it has a fixed number of things in it.

This painting set has 10 paints and a paintbrush.

a scarf set, with matching hat, scarf and gloves

a set of "tens" numbers

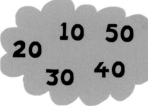

10 50
20
30 40

Fractions

A fraction is a part of something. Fractions can be part of one thing, or part of a group of things.

Fractions on number lines

You can find fractions on a number line.

0            $6\frac{1}{2}$ 10

Divide equally

To divide something equally, you split it into parts or groups of the same size or number.

This pizza has been divided equally into four pieces. Each piece is the same size.

These carrots have been divided equally into two groups. Each group has the same number of carrots in it.

Equal parts

Equal parts are the same size or numbers as each other.

The parts of this window are equal – they are the same size.

This group of 6 bottles has been divided into parts that are equal by number – there are 3 bottles in each part.

Unequal parts

Unequal parts are different sizes or numbers from each other.

The parts of this window are unequal – they are not the same size.

This group of 6 bottles has been divided into unequal parts by number – there is a different number of bottles in each part.

Whole

A thing or group of things you are going to divide into fractions is called a whole.

Before you divide them up, each of these can be called a whole.

a shape, such as a star

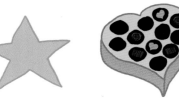

a piece of cheese

a collection of things, such as chocolates

Even half a melon can be called a whole when you are going to divide it up.

Whole numbers

A whole number is not a fraction.

These are whole numbers.

9 26 0 11

These are fractions.

$\frac{1}{2}$ $\frac{3}{4}$ $\frac{2}{3}$ $\frac{1}{4}$

These are whole numbers and fractions.

$6\frac{3}{4}$ $8\frac{1}{2}$ $21\frac{1}{3}$

Halves

When you halve something you split it into two equal parts called halves. Each part is one half. You write a half like this: $\frac{1}{2}$.

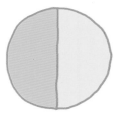

This circle is split into halves.

$\frac{1}{2}$ of this square is striped.

$\frac{1}{2}$ of this triangle is spotted.

The whole rectangle is yellow.

Half an apple is half of a whole apple.

3 out of 6, or half, of these apples are red.

Two halves are the same as a whole.

Thirds

When you split something into three equal parts, the parts are called thirds. You write a third like this: $\frac{1}{3}$.

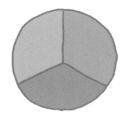

This circle is split into thirds.

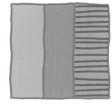

$\frac{1}{3}$ of this square is striped.

$\frac{2}{3}$ of this triangle is spotted.

The whole rectangle is green.

2 out of 6, or one third, of these hens are sitting down. 4 out of 6, or two thirds, of them have laid an egg.

Three thirds are the same as a whole.

Quarters

When you split something into four equal parts, the parts are called quarters. You write a quarter like this: $\frac{1}{4}$.

This circle is split into quarters.

$\frac{1}{4}$ of this square is striped.

$\frac{2}{4}$ of this square is spotted. $\frac{2}{4}$ is the same as $\frac{1}{2}$.

The whole rectangle is blue.

3 out of 12, or one quarter, of these flowers are pink.

6 flowers, or two quarters (half) of them, are yellow.

9 out of 12, or three quarters of them, have 5 petals.

Four quarters are the same as a whole.

Find out more about: equals (page 41)

Adding and subtracting

Adding and subtracting do the opposite of each other. Adding puts together amounts. Subtracting takes away amounts, or finds the difference between them.

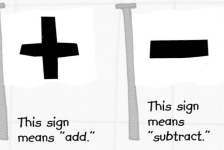

This sign means "add."

This sign means "subtract."

Addition

There are two ways to think about addition.

1. It means putting together two or more amounts.

2. It also means making an amount bigger by adding to it.

You can find out more about this on pages 57 and 58.

Plus

Plus means add. 2 plus 3 means "add 2 and 3."

The plus sign is a short way of telling you to add. It looks like this: **+**

2 + 3

2 + 3 means "2 add 3."
(The answer is 5.)

Increase

When you increase something you make it bigger.

Make

In addition, make (or makes) is another way of saying "equals." So "2 and 2 make 4" means the same as "2 add 2 equals 4." Or you can write 2 + 2 = 4.

Sum

The new number or amount that you make when you add is called the sum. Another word for sum is total.

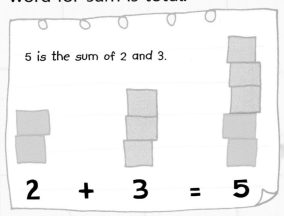

5 is the sum of 2 and 3.

2   +   3   =   5

Number sentences

Addition

An addition sentence describes adding. You can write addition sentences in different ways.

You can use words:

Three plus two is five.

Or words and numbers:

3 and 2 equals 5.

Or use numbers and signs:

3 + 2 = 5
You can also write: 5 = 3 + 2

Subtraction

A subtraction sentence describes subtracting. You can write subtraction sentences in different ways.

You can use words:

Eight minus five is three.

Or words and numbers:

8 take away 5 equals 3.

Or use numbers and signs:

8 – 5 = 3
You can also write: 3 = 8 – 5

Putting together

Adding is putting two numbers or amounts together and finding out how many there are altogether. The new number or amount is called the sum or the total.

Ella has a bag of 5 pieces of candy.　　Isaac has a bag of 3 candies.

If they pour all their candies into another bag, then count them, they find out how many candies there are altogether.

You can write this as a number sentence:

5 + 3 = 8

Here are some "putting together" words you may see.

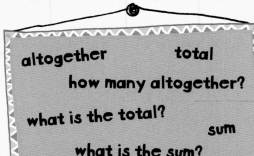

altogether　　total
how many altogether?
what is the total?
sum
what is the sum?

Making bigger

Adding to a number or amount makes it bigger. Another word for this is increasing. When you increase, you have an amount already and you add more to it.

Arthur has 6 candies.

Bea gives him 4 more.

Now Arthur has 10 candies.

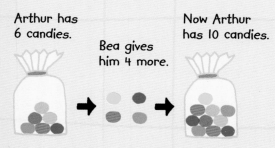

You can show this on a number line by finding the number you want to add to, and counting up.

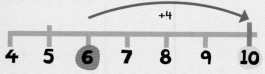

You start at 6 (for the 6 candies Arthur has) then count up 4 more.

You can write this as a number sentence:

$$6 + 4 = 10$$

Here are some "increasing" words you may see.

count forward   count up

more   increase by   go up by

how many more to make ...?

how much more is ...?

how many more is ... than ...?

Doubling

Adding a number to itself, such as 2 + 2, is called doubling. You can find out more about doubles on page 67.

Order of addition

You can add numbers in any order. The answer is the same.

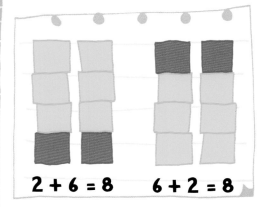

$$2 + 6 = 8 \qquad 6 + 2 = 8$$

You can see this on a number line too.

To add 2 + 6, you can start at 2 and count up 6...

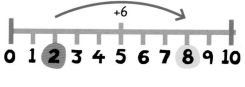

Or start at 6 and count up 2.

Whichever way you add 2 and 6, the answer is the same: 8.

Subtraction

There are four ways to think about subtraction.

1. It is taking away an amount.

2. It is making a number or amount smaller by taking something away from it.

3. It is finding the difference between two amounts.

4. It is also separating an amount into two other amounts.

You can find out more about this on pages 59 to 61.

Decrease

Decreasing something makes it smaller.

Minus

Minus means subtract. 4 minus 3 means "subtract 3 from 4."

The minus sign is a short way of telling you to subtract. It looks like this: **—**

4 − 3

4 − 3 means "subtract 3 from 4," or "4 take away 3." (The answer is 1.)

Leave

In subtraction, leave (or leaves) is another way to say "equals." So "5 take away 3 leaves 2" means the same as "5 minus 3 equals 2." Or you can write 5 − 3 = 2.

Taking away

Subtracting is taking one number or amount away from another one and finding out how many there are left.

Philip has 9 candies.

He gives 4 to Emily.

Now Philip has 5 candies left.

You can write this as a number sentence:

9 − 4 = 5

Here are some "taking away" words you may see.

take away

leave/leaves

remove

remaining

how many are left /left over?

Making smaller

Subtracting is making an amount smaller. Another word for this is decreasing.

The price for a sucker is reduced by 4¢ from 20¢. You can count back from 20¢ to find the new price (16¢).

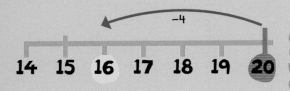

You can show this on a number line by finding the number you want to make smaller (20), and counting back.

You can write this as a number sentence:

20 − 4 = 16

Here are some "decreasing" words you may see.

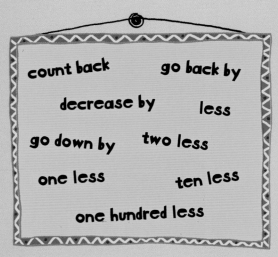

count back   go back by

decrease by   less

go down by   two less

one less   ten less

one hundred less

Finding the difference

Subtracting is comparing two amounts or numbers. This means looking at them and finding the difference between them. This is not the same as "taking away subtraction" because nothing is being moved.

Harry has 7 marbles.

Kal has 4.

The difference between 7 and 4 is 3. You can say that Harry has 3 more marbles than Kal. Kal has 3 fewer marbles than Harry.

You can write this as a number sentence:

7 − 4 = 3

Here are some "comparing" words you may see.

difference between

how many fewer is ... than...?

how much less is ... than ...?

what is the difference?

how many more?

how many fewer?

how much greater?

how much less?

Separating

Subtracting is separating an amount or number into other amounts or numbers. Another name for this is partitioning.

| Abigail has 14 candies in a bag. | She puts 6 candies in one bag... | ...and puts 8 candies into another bag. |

Abigail has not taken any of the candies away (there are still 14 candies), but she has separated them into two bags.

You can write this as a number sentence:

$$14 = 6 + 8$$
or $$14 - 8 = 6$$
or $$14 - 6 = 8$$

Here are some "separating" words you may see.

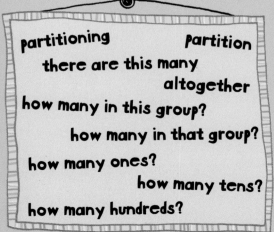

partitioning   partition

there are this many

altogether

how many in this group?

how many in that group?

how many ones?

how many tens?

how many hundreds?

It is sometimes useful to partition a number by place value.

14 is the same as one ten and 4 ones, so you can write:

$$14 = 10 + 4$$

127 is the same as one hundred, 2 tens and 7 ones, so you can write:

$$127 = 100 + 20 + 7$$

Halving

Separating something into two amounts that are the same size is called halving. When you halve something, each part is called a half.

Each part of this cake is the same size, so the pieces are halves.

There are 10 candles. They can be separated into 2 groups of 5, so 5 is half of 10.

$$10 = 5 + 5$$

Order of subtraction

You can't do subtraction in any order, because you will get different answers. 5 − 2 is not the same as 2 − 5.

Find out more about: halves (fractions) (page 54); halving (page 82)

Useful opposites

Adding and subtracting do the opposite of each other. You undo an addition by subtracting and you undo a subtraction by adding.

3 + 2 = 5

5 − 2 = 3

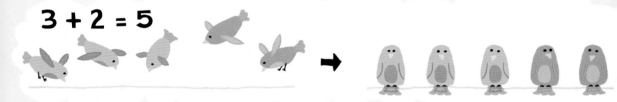

3 + 2 = 5

5 − 2 = 3

When you know an addition fact,
you can find out subtraction facts too.

So when you know: you also know that: and that:

3 + 2 = 5 **5 − 2 = 3** **5 − 3 = 2**

When you know a subtraction fact, you can find out related addition facts.

Adding and subtracting odd and even numbers

You can tell before you add or subtract if the answer will be odd or even.

These Numicon shapes show what happens when you add odd and even numbers.

$4 + 2 = 6$

even + even = even

$3 + 5 = 8$

odd + odd = even

$3 + 2 = 5$

odd + even = odd

You can add numbers in any order so **even + odd = odd**

$2 + 3 = 5$

These Numicon shapes show what happens when you subtract odd and even numbers.

$6 - 2 = 4$

even - even = even

$8 - 5 = 3$

even - odd = odd

$5 - 3 = 2$

odd - odd = even

$5 - 2 = 3$

odd - even = odd

Numicon is published by Oxford University Press and Numicon materials are reproduced with their permission.

Adding and subtracting using number lines

You can use number lines to help you add and subtract. (Pages 25 and 28 to 30 tell you more about how to count on number lines.)

When you add on a number line, you hop, step or jump to the right.

For 5 + 3   Count up 3.

Start at 5.

When you subtract on a number line, you hop, step or jump to the left.

For 16 – 4   Start at 16, then count back 4.

0 1 2 3 4 **5** 6 7 **8** 9 10 11 **12** 13 14 15 **16** 17 18 19 20

As you learn addition and subtraction pairs, you can take larger jumps, such as 2s, 3s, 4s and 5s, to find your answers more quickly.

11 + 4
When you know that 1 + 4 = 5, you can jump forward 4 from 11 to see that 11 + 4 = 15.

29 – 3
When you know that 9 – 3 = 6, you can jump back 3 from 29 to see that 29 – 3 = 26.

+4   –3

10 **11** 12 13 14 **15** 16 17 18 19 20 21 22 23 24 25 **26** 27 28 **29** 30

Sometimes it helps to add a number in two stages by "bouncing off a ten." Count forward to a number that ends with a 0, then "bounce off" the "tens" number to add any more you need. For subtraction, count back to a "tens" number then "bounce off" it backward.

27 + 8
Start adding 8 by jumping up 3 from 27 to 30. 8 = 3 + 5 so now you need to bounce off the 30 and count up 5 more. So 27 + 8 = 35.

46 – 8
Start taking away 8 by jumping back 6 from 46 to 40. 8 = 6 + 2 so now you need to count back 2 more. So 46 – 8 = 38.

+3   +5   –2   –6

20   **25** **27** 30   **35**   **38** 40   45**46**   **50**

Find out more about: addition and subtraction pairs (pages 66-68); left (page 102); right (page 102); "tens" numbers (page 34)

Sometimes it can help to add a number by bouncing off 5s. First count up to a number that ends with a 5, then "bounce off" the 5 number to add any more you need. For subtraction, you count back to a 5 number then "bounce off" it backward.

33 + 6
You can start adding 6 by jumping up 2 from 33 to 35, but 6 = 2 + 4 so now you need to count up 4 more. So 33 + 6 = 39.

49 – 6
You can start taking away 6 by jumping back 4 from 49 to 45, but 6 = 4 + 2 so now you need to count back 2 more. So 49 – 6 = 43.

+2   +4   –2   –4

30 31 32 **33** 34 ⟨35⟩ 36 37 38 39 40 41 42 43 44 ⟨45⟩ 46 47 48 49 50

Crossing tens boundaries

A tens boundary is where the tens digit changes, for example from teen numbers to twenties, or from thirties to forties. You can add a number in two stages to cross tens boundaries.

The tens boundaries on this number line are shown in pink circles.

40 is the boundary between thirties and forties numbers.

0   10   20   30   40   50   60

Adding using addition squares

To use an addition square to add:

1. In the top row, find one of the numbers you want to add and draw a straight line down.

2. In the first column, find the number you want to add to it and draw a straight line across.

3. The answer is the number where the two lines meet.

+	0	1	2	3	4	5	6
0	0	1	2	3	4	5	6
1	1	2	3	4	5	6	7
2	2	3	4	5	6	7	8
3	3	4	5	6	7	8	9
4	4	5	6	7	8	9	10
5	5	6	7	8	9	10	11
6	6	7	8	9	10	11	12

This is a 0 to 6 addition square. To add 4 + 3, draw lines down from 4 and across from 3. The lines meet at 7: 4 + 3 = 7.

Addition pairs

An addition pair is two numbers that you add together. Adding each pair of numbers always gives the same total.

3 + 2 = 5

Three and two is always five, never four or two.

You can do addition in any order: the answer is the same.

3 + 2 = 5
2 + 3 = 5

Adding 3 + 2 is the same as adding 2 + 3.

Learning some simple addition pairs will help you quickly add all sorts of numbers.

Subtraction pairs

Addition and subtraction are opposites, so knowing addition pairs will help you find out subtraction pairs.

2 + 3 = 5

so

5 – 2 = 3

and

5 – 3 = 2

Remember, you can't subtract in any order. 5 – 3 is not the same as 3 – 5. You always take the second number from the first.

Pairs up to 5

First you need to learn the pairs that make small numbers, such as 1 + 1 = 2, for all the numbers up to 5.

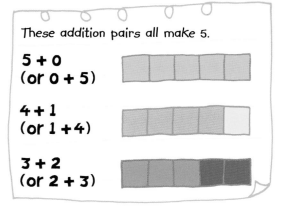

These addition pairs all make 5.

5 + 0
(or 0 + 5)

4 + 1
(or 1 + 4)

3 + 2
(or 2 + 3)

Pairs that make 10

This grid shows pairs of numbers that make 10.

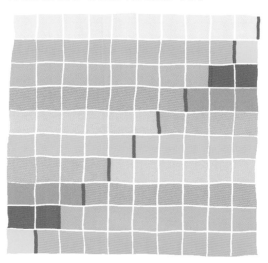

You can write the pairs that make 10 as addition sentences.

10 + 0 = 10
9 + 1 = 10 and so on

Another way of showing pairs of numbers that make 10 is using an abacus.

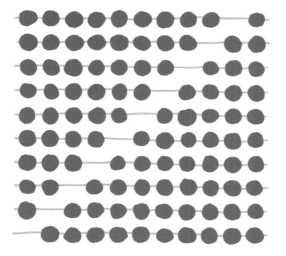

Once you know the pairs that make 10, you can use them to find related subtraction pairs.

$1 + 9 = 10$ *so* $10 - 9 = 1$
$2 + 8 = 10$ *so* $10 - 8 = 2$
and so on — *and so on*

Doubles

A number added to itself gives a double. Doubles of whole numbers are even numbers.

Here are the doubles of the numbers from 1 to 10.

$1 + 1 = 2$	$6 + 6 = 12$
$2 + 2 = 4$	$7 + 7 = 14$
$3 + 3 = 6$	$8 + 8 = 16$
$4 + 4 = 8$	$9 + 9 = 18$
$5 + 5 = 10$	$10 + 10 = 20$

Near doubles

Near doubles or "next door numbers" are "double add 1." $(3 + 4 = 3 + 3 + 1 = 7)$ It can help you work out answers quickly if you can spot near doubles at a glance.

Here are some near doubles that are easy to figure out.

$3 + 4 = 7$
$4 + 5 = 9$
$6 + 7 = 13$
$7 + 8 = 15$

Pairs that make 20

Adding to 20 uses the same digits as when you add to 10, but you just need to remember the 10 in front of it.

This blue area represents 10.

One more square is added to make 11, 2 more make 12, and so on.

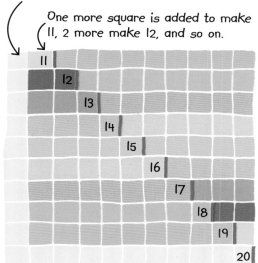

The pairs that make 20 are:
$11 + 9 = 20$
$12 + 8 = 20$ *and so on*

Find out more about: digits (page 9); doubling (page 79)

Pairs that make 100

You can use the pairs that make 10 to help you find pairs that make 100.

Each square represents 10.

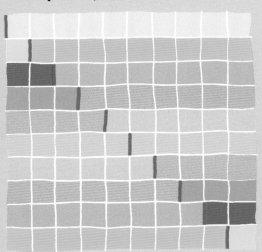

These pairs of numbers all add up to 100. Each number is a multiple of 10.

0	and	100
10	and	90
20	and	80
30	and	70
40	and	60
50	and	50
60	and	40
70	and	30
80	and	20
90	and	10
100	and	0

You can write the pairs as addition sentences, and find out related subtraction pairs too.

$10 + 90 = 100$ so $100 - 90 = 10$
$20 + 80 = 100$ so $100 - 80 = 20$
and so on   and so on

Adding and subtracting 0

When you add or subtract 0, the number does not change.

$13 + 0 = 13$
$29 + 0 = 29$
and so on

Any number + 0 is itself.

$8 - 0 = 8$
$32 - 0 = 32$
and so on

Any number – 0 is itself.

Adding and subtracting 1

Look at the squares from left to right to see what happens when you add 1 each time.

- - - - - - - - - - - - - - ->

The pale yellow squares show what you add to 5 to make the numbers from 6 to 10. For example, $7 = 5 + 2$.

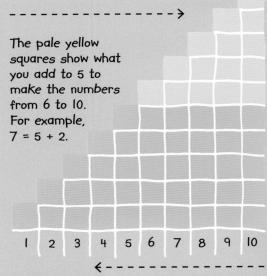

| 1 | 2 | 3 | 4 | 5 | 6 | 7 | 8 | 9 | 10 |

<- - - - - - - - - - - - - -

Look at the squares from right to left to see what happens when you subtract 1 each time.

Adding and subtracting 2

Adding 2 to an even number gives the next even number along the number line. Adding 2 to an odd number gives the next odd number along.

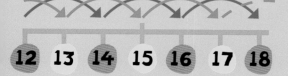

Subtracting 2 from an even number gives the next even number back along the line. Subtracting 2 from an odd number gives the next odd number back.

Mental addition and subtraction

When you do a calculation, work out as much as you can in your head. It is usually quicker, and you can use any method you like. It is fine to jot down numbers as you go to help you remember them.

Adding and subtracting ten

When you add 10, think of jumping ten places forward along a number line.

The tens digit of 32 is 1 (one ten) bigger than 22, and the ones digit is the same.

To subtract 10, think of jumping ten places backward along a number line.

The tens digit of 35 is 1 (one ten) smaller than 45, and the ones digit is the same.

Adding and subtracting multiples of ten

To add and subtract multiples of 10, think of jumping along the number line in tens.

Jump forward to add multiples of 10, for example to add 21 + 30, jump 3 sets of 10.

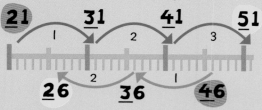

Jump back in 10s to subtract multiples of 10. To do 46 − 20, jump back 2 sets of 10.

Find out more about: calculations (page 88); counting on number lines (page 25); counting on number lines: in twos (page 28), in tens (page 30); multiples of 10 (pages 34-35)

Adding and subtracting near tens

Once you can add and subtract "tens" numbers, you can use what you know to help you subtract "near tens" numbers, such as 9 or 11, or 19 or 21.

To add or subtract 9 or 11, you add or subtract 10 and then adjust your answer.

To add **17 + 9**
do **17 + 10** then subtract 1
= **27 − 1**
= **26**

To subtract **27 − 11**
do **27 − 10** then subtract another 1
= **17 − 1**
= **16**

To add or subtract 19 or 21, you add or subtract 20 and then adjust your answer.

To add **26 + 19**
do **26 + 20** then subtract 1
= **46 − 1**
= **45**
and so on

Adding near doubles

When two numbers are nearly the same size, you can use their doubles to help you add them.

You can double the bigger number and take away the difference. Or you can double the smaller number and add the difference.

To add **5 + 6** you can double the 5 and add 1 (the difference between them)
5 + 5 = 10
10 + 1 = 11
or you could double the 6 and subtract 1.
6 + 6 − 1 = 11

To add **6 + 7**
you could double the 6 and add 1:
6 + 6 = 12
12 + 1 = 13
or you could double the 7 and subtract 1.
7 + 7 − 1 = 13

Double the number you find easier, then adjust the answer.

To add **24 + 25**
you could double the 25 and take away 1:
25 + 25 − 1 = 49

To add **25 + 26**
you would double the 25 and add 1:
25 + 25 + 1 = 51

Find out more about: difference (page 60); doubles (page 67); doubling (page 79); near doubles (page 67); "tens" numbers (page 34)

Splitting up numbers

Some questions are easier to do if you split the numbers into smaller numbers, and add or subtract in stages.

Sometimes it is useful to split a number into 5 and a part.

$$8 + 6$$
$$= 5 + 3 + 5 + 1$$
$$= 10 + 4$$
$$= 14$$

Or you might want to split a number into 10 and a part.

$$17 + 12$$
$$= 17 + 10 + 2$$
$$= 27 + 2$$
$$= 29$$

$$29 - 13$$
$$= 29 - 10 - 3$$
$$= 19 - 3$$
$$= 16$$

It may help to split a number into a double and a part.

$$12 + 17$$
$$= 12 + 12 + 5$$
$$= 24 + 5$$
$$= 29$$

Adding three numbers

You can add numbers in any order, so choose the order carefully, to make the adding as easy as you can.

Look for pairs that make life easier for you.

To add $11 + 2 + 9$

add $11 + 9$ to make a "tens" number

$$11 + 9 = 20$$

Then add 2 to find the answer.

$$20 + 2 = 22$$

To add $12 + 3 + 13$

12 and 13 are near doubles, so you could add them first:

$$12 + 13 = 25 \quad (12 + 12 + 1)$$

Then add 3 to find the answer.

$$25 + 3 = 28$$

If you can't see a useful pair of numbers, it often helps to put the largest numbers first.

To add $5 + 8 + 21$

do $21 + 8 + 5$
$$= 29 + 5$$
$$= 34$$

You can use the same methods to add longer lists of numbers too.

Find out more about: doubles (page 67); "tens" numbers (page 34)

Adding and subtracting using place value

You can use what you know about place value to add and subtract numbers.

If you know $2 + 7 = 9$

then you know $20 + 70 = 90$

If you know $9 - 1 = 8$

then you know $90 - 10 = 80$

Missing numbers

Missing number problems tell you two numbers in a number sentence and leave you to find the third. To work out the answer, it helps to remember that addition and subtraction are opposites.

To do:

$\square + 3 = 7$

you could use:

$7 - 3 = \square$

To do:

$5 + \square = 9$

you could use:

$9 - 5 = \square$

Word problems

When you read a word problem, it can often help to write down the math you need to do as a missing number problem.

Don't know the result

There are 2 beetles sitting on a leaf. 3 beetles land on another leaf. How many beetles are there altogether?

$2 + 3 = \boxed{?}$

$2 + 3 = \boxed{5}$

You can answer this question with number facts you know ($2 + 3 = 5$).

There are 5 eggs. 3 eggs hatch out. How many eggs are left?

$5 - 3 = \boxed{?}$

$5 - 3 = \boxed{2}$

You can answer this question with number facts you know ($5 - 3 = 2$).

Don't know the starting number

A dog buries 3 bones in a hole in the ground, on top of some bones he buried earlier. Now there are 7 bones in the hole. How many were there already?

$\boxed{?} + 3 = 7$
$\boxed{4} + 3 = 7$

You can answer this question with number facts you know (4 + 3 = 7).

Or you can use opposites:
The opposite of +3 is −3.
7 − 3 = 4, so the missing number is 4.

A dog buries some bones. He digs up 3 and there are 4 still in the ground. How many were there to start with?

$\boxed{?} - 3 = 4$
$\boxed{7} - 3 = 4$

You can answer this question with number facts you know (7 − 3 = 4).

Or you can use opposites:
The opposite of −3 is +3.
4 + 3 = 7, so there were 7 bones.

Don't know the number that is added

Pirate Pat puts 12 gold coins into a treasure chest. Pirate Peggy puts hers in. Now there are 29 coins in the chest. How many did Pirate Peggy add?

$12 + \boxed{?} = 29$

You can count forward to find the answer: 12 and 10 is 22, and 7 more is 29, so the number you would write in the box is 17.

Or you can use opposites: take Pat's coins out of the chest to find out how many Peggy put in. 29 − 12 = 17, so the answer is 17.

There are 29 gold coins in a chest. Pirate Peggy took some out. There are 12 left. How many did she take?

$29 - \boxed{?} = 12$
$29 - \boxed{17} = 12$

You can use near tens and opposites to solve this problem quickly.
Use 30 − 12 − 1 = 17, so Peggy took 17.

Find out more about: counting forward (page 26); adding and subtracting near tens (page 70); opposites (page 62)

73

Checking calculations

It is easy to make mistakes with numbers. (Everyone does it.) It's best to check your calculation by doing it again a different way. Check that the answer makes sense too.

Use opposites

Addition and subtraction are opposites, and you can use this to help check your answers.

To check
17 + 8 = 25
try
25 − 8 = 17

This calculation works with the same numbers, so your answer is correct.

To check
22 − 7 = 15
try
15 + 7 = 22

This calculation works with the same numbers, so your answer is correct.

Use near doubles or near tens

See page 67 to find out how to use near doubles, and page 70 to read about near tens.

Use number facts

You can often use number facts to help you check an answer, or part of it.

To check
29 − 17 = 12
you could try
20 − 10 = 10
and
9 − 7 = 2
so
10 + 2 = 12

Change the order

You can check addition by adding the numbers in a different order.

To check
14 + 6 + 8 = 28
try
14 + 8 + 6 = 28

The sum is the same so the answer is correct.

Using a calculator

You can use a calculator to add or subtract numbers, or to check your answers. Pages 88 to 89 show you how.

Multiplying and dividing

Multiplying and dividing are opposites. Multiplying is counting in equal groups. Dividing is separating a quantity into equal groups.

This sign means "multiply."

This sign means "divide."

Multiplication

There are three ways to think about multiplication.

1. It is counting in groups: adding up several sets of the same number or amount.

2. You can picture it as an array: for example 4 rows of stickers with 3 stickers in each row.

These stamps are arranged in an array.

3. Multiplication also means scaling: such as 5 times as heavy or 3 times as long.

You can find out more about multiplication on pages 76-77.

Times

Times is another way to say multiply. 2 times 3 means count in groups of 2 three times. (2 + 2 + 2) So 2 x 3 means multiply 2 three times.

The multiplication sign is a short way of telling you to multiply. It looks like this: **X**

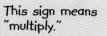

2 x 3   2 x 3 means "2 multiplied by 3." (2 x 3 is 6.)

Product

The new number or amount that you make when you multiply is called the product.

6 is the product of 2 and 3.

2   x   3   =   6

2 times 3 means 3 groups of 2.

Find out more about: equal (page 41)

Multiplication sentences

Multiplication sentences describe multiplying. You can write them in different ways. You can use words:

> **Five multiplied by two is ten.**

Or words and numbers:

> **5 times 2 equals 10.**

Or use numbers and signs:

> **5 x 2 = 10**

You can also write: 10 = 5 x 2
Don't forget that 5 x 2 means counting in 5s twice. (This is different from 2 x 5, which is counting in 2s five times.)

Multiples

A multiple is the number you make when you multiply one number by another.

2 x 2 = 4

2 x 3 = 6

4 and 6 are both multiples of 2.

You can find out more about multiples on pages 34 and 35.

Repeated adding

Multiplying means repeated adding. So multiplying something by 3 is the same as adding 3 groups of it together.

Each starfish has five arms.

To find out how many arms they have altogether you multiply 5 by 3.
You can write this as a number sentence:

> **5 x 3 = 15**

The answer is the same as:

> **5 + 5 + 5 = 15**

Repeated adding is the opposite of repeated subtracting.

Here are some "repeated adding" words you may see.

> so many sets of
>
> how many groups of?
>
> how many altogether?
>
> sets of
>
> groups of

Arrays

An array is a group of things set out in rows and columns. There is the same number of things in each row and the same number in each column.

To find out how many things are in an array, multiply the number of rows by the number of things in a row.

There are 4 rows of cookies. There are 5 cookies in each row.

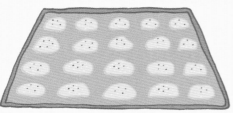

To find out how many cookies there are altogether, multiply 5 by 4. You can write this as a number sentence:

5 x 4 = 20

You can also multiply the number of columns by the number of things in a column.

There are 5 columns of cookies, with 4 cookies in each column, so you could also multiply 4 by 5.

4 x 5 = 20

"Array" words include:

row   column

Scaling

Scaling is making something a number of times bigger or smaller. When you scale something, remember to multiply each part of it.

To decorate this gingerbread man you need:

- 2 chocolate chip eyes
- 1 cherry candy smile
- 3 white chocolate chip buttons

To decorate 2 gingerbread men you need twice as many of each kind of candy:

- 4 chocolate chip eyes (2 x 2)
- 2 cherry candy smiles (1 x 2)
- 6 white chocolate chip buttons (3 x 2)

Here are some "scaling" words you may see.

multiplied by   times as large
for every   times as big
for each
times as much
double (x2)
triple (x3)
twice (x2)

Find out more about: columns (page 32); rows (page 32)

Counting up in groups

Multiplying is counting up in groups.

You can multiply groups of two. 10 groups of 2 is 20.

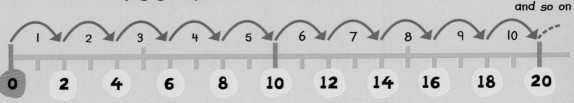

You can multiply groups of three. 10 groups of 3 is 30.

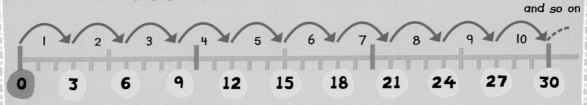

You can multiply groups of four. 10 groups of 4 is 40.

You can multiply groups of five. 10 groups of 5 is 50.

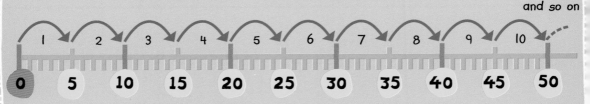

You can multiply groups of ten. 10 groups of 10 is 100.

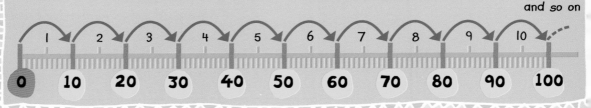

Doubling

Doubling any number multiplies it by 2. The double of any whole number is an even number.

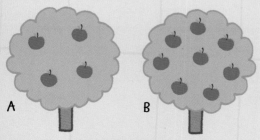

A   B

Tree B has double the number of apples on it as tree A. 8 is twice 4.

$$4 \times 2 = 8$$

Here are the doubles of the numbers from 1 to 10.

$1 \times 2 = 2$ $6 \times 2 = 12$
$2 \times 2 = 4$ $7 \times 2 = 14$
$3 \times 2 = 6$ $8 \times 2 = 16$
$4 \times 2 = 8$ $9 \times 2 = 18$
$5 \times 2 = 10$ $10 \times 2 = 20$

"Doubling" words include:

double   twice
          two times
same again   two sets of

Doubling is the opposite of halving. You can find out more about halving on page 82.

Order of multiplication

You can multiply numbers in any order. The answer is the same.

$$3 \times 2 = 6$$

$$2 \times 3 = 6$$

You can see this on a number line too.

To multiply 2×3, you can start at 0 and count up 3 sets of 2...

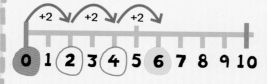

...or start at 0 and count up 2 sets of 3.

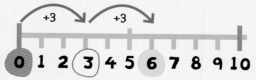

Whichever way you do it, the answer is the same: 6.

Find out more about: doubles (page 67), doubling (page 58); whole numbers (page 54)

Division

There are two ways to think about division.

1. It is sharing into equal groups.

2. It is reducing a quantity by equal amounts, by repeated subtraction.

Division sign

The division sign is a short way of telling you to divide. It looks like this: ÷

$$8 \div 2$$ 8 ÷ 2 means "8 divided by 2." (8 ÷ 2 is 4.)

Factors

A factor is a number that divides exactly into another one.

You can divide 8 into 4 groups of 2, and 2 groups of 4, so 2 and 4 are both factors of 8.

Order of division

You can't do division in any order, because you will get different answers. 8 ÷ 2 is not the same as 2 ÷ 8.

Division sentences

Division sentences describe dividing. You can write them in different ways.

You can use words:

Six divided by three is two.

Or words and numbers:

6 divided by 3 equals 2.

Or use numbers and signs:

$$6 \div 3 = 2$$

You can also write: 2 = 6 ÷ 3

Remainders

Sometimes when you divide, you have something left over. This is the remainder.

If you divide 8 ducklings into groups of 3, you will have 2 groups, and 2 ducklings left. This is the remainder.

"Remainder" words include:

left   left over
how many left?

Find out more about: equal (page 41); exactly (page 41); subtracting (page 59)

Sharing

Dividing is sharing an amount out so every share is the same size.

Jay and Maya are given a pack of 20 crayons to share. How many do they each get?

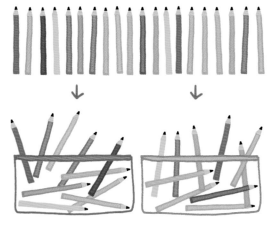

To find out how many crayons each child gets, divide 20 by 2. (They each get 10 crayons.)

You can write this as a number sentence:

20 ÷ 2 = 10

Here are some "sharing" words you might see:

sharing share between

shared equally between

fair how many each?

the same as each

one each, two each, ...

Grouping

Dividing is putting things in groups of the same size, to see how many groups there are.

Beth has a sheet of 12 stickers. She wants to give 3 each to her friends. How many friends can she give stickers to?

To find out how many of Beth's friends would get stickers, divide 12 by 3.

You can write this as a number sentence:

12 ÷ 3 = 4

Grouping is repeated subtracting. It is the opposite of repeated adding.

You can show this on a number line.

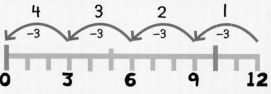

These words tell you to divide an amount into groups:

how many groups / groups of

how many sets / sets of

equal groups of

group in pairs, twos, threes...

Find out more about: adding (pages 56-58); subtracting (page 59)

Halving

Halving any number divides it by 2.

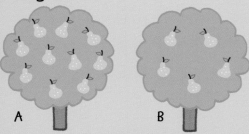

A   B

Tree B has half as many pears on it as tree A. 5 is half of 10.

$$10 \div 2 = 5$$

Here are the halves of the even numbers up to 20.

$$2 \div 2 = 1 \qquad 12 \div 2 = 6$$
$$4 \div 2 = 2 \qquad 14 \div 2 = 7$$
$$6 \div 2 = 3 \qquad 16 \div 2 = 8$$
$$8 \div 2 = 4 \qquad 18 \div 2 = 9$$
$$10 \div 2 = 5 \qquad 20 \div 2 = 10$$

"Halving words" include:

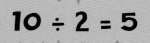

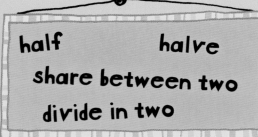

half   halve

share between two

divide in two

Halving is the opposite of doubling. You can read more about doubling on page 79.

Useful opposites

Multiplying and dividing are opposites. You undo multiplication by dividing, and you undo division by multiplying.

Reuben, Zach and Ethan made 2 handprints each. How many handprints altogether?

$$2 \times 3 = 6$$

Some children made 2 handprints each. There are 6 handprints. How many children?

$$6 \div 2 = 3$$

You can use multiplication facts to find out related division facts.

So when you know: $2 \times 6 = 12$

You also know that: $12 \div 2 = 6$

and that: $12 \div 6 = 2$

You can use division facts to find out multiplication facts.

So when you know: $15 \div 3 = 5$

You also know that: $5 \times 3 = 15$

Times tables

Times tables are lists of multiplication facts. Learning them helps you do calculations quickly. There are times tables for all the numbers up to 12, but you start by learning the tables for 2, 5, 10, 4 and 3.

2x table

2 × 1 = 2
2 × 2 = 4
2 × 3 = 6
2 × 4 = 8
2 × 5 = 10
2 × 6 = 12
2 × 7 = 14
2 × 8 = 16
2 × 9 = 18
2 × 10 = 20

4x table

4 × 1 = 4
4 × 2 = 8
4 × 3 = 12
4 × 4 = 16
4 × 5 = 20
4 × 6 = 24
4 × 7 = 28
4 × 8 = 32
4 × 9 = 36
4 × 10 = 40

3x table

3 × 1 = 3
3 × 2 = 6
3 × 3 = 9
3 × 4 = 12
3 × 5 = 15
3 × 6 = 18
3 × 7 = 21
3 × 8 = 24
3 × 9 = 27
3 × 10 = 30

5x table

5 × 1 = 5
5 × 2 = 10
5 × 3 = 15
5 × 4 = 20
5 × 5 = 25
5 × 6 = 30
5 × 7 = 35
5 × 8 = 40
5 × 9 = 45
5 × 10 = 50

The 10x table and hints on learning times tables are on page 84.

Find out more about: calculations (page 88)

10x table

$$10 \times 1 = 10$$
$$10 \times 2 = 20$$
$$10 \times 3 = 30$$
$$10 \times 4 = 40$$
$$10 \times 5 = 50$$
$$10 \times 6 = 60$$
$$10 \times 7 = 70$$
$$10 \times 8 = 80$$
$$10 \times 9 = 90$$
$$10 \times 10 = 100$$

Learning times tables

One way to learn times tables is to say them steadily over and over again. This is called reciting. Here are some ways you could recite the 2x table.

Two times one is two.
Two times two is four.
Two times three is six.
and so on

Two ones are two.
Two twos are four.
Two threes are six.
and so on

One two is two.
Two twos are four.
Three twos are six.
and so on

Multiplication facts on number grids

When you show multiples of numbers on a number grid, you can start to see patterns.

These hundred grids show the patterns that the multiples of 2 and 5 make. The patterns for the multiples of 3, 4 and 10 are on page 35.

Multiples of 2 are all even numbers. They end in 2, 4, 6, 8 or 0.

1	2	3	4	5	6	7	8	9	10
11	12	13	14	15	16	17	18	19	20
21	22	23	24	25	26	27	28	29	30
31	32	33	34	35	36	37	38	39	40
41	42	43	44	45	46	47	48	49	50
51	52	53	54	55	56	57	58	59	60
61	62	63	64	65	66	67	68	69	70
71	72	73	74	75	76	77	78	79	80
81	82	83	84	85	86	87	88	89	90
91	92	93	94	95	96	97	98	99	100

Multiples of 5 all end in 5 or 0.

1	2	3	4	5	6	7	8	9	10
11	12	13	14	15	16	17	18	19	20
21	22	23	24	25	26	27	28	29	30
31	32	33	34	35	36	37	38	39	40
41	42	43	44	45	46	47	48	49	50
51	52	53	54	55	56	57	58	59	60
61	62	63	64	65	66	67	68	69	70
71	72	73	74	75	76	77	78	79	80
81	82	83	84	85	86	87	88	89	90
91	92	93	94	95	96	97	98	99	100

Multiplying and dividing using place value

You can use what you know about place value to help you multiply and divide numbers.

If you know: **8 x 3 = 24**

then you know: **80 x 3 = 240**

If you know: **12 ÷ 2 = 6**

then you know: **120 ÷ 20 = 6**

Missing numbers

Missing number problems give you two numbers in a number sentence and leave you to find the third. To work out the answer, it helps to remember that multiplication and division are opposites.

To do:

☐ **x 3 = 15**

you could use:

15 ÷ 3 = ☐

To do:

4 x ☐ **= 16**

you could use:

16 ÷ 4 = ☐

Word problems

When you read a word problem, it can often help to write down the math you need to do as a missing number problem.

Don't know the result

There are 6 Easter eggs in a package. Georgie has 2 packages. How many eggs are there altogether?

6 x 2 = ?

6 x 2 = 12

You can answer this question with number facts you know (6 x 2 = 12).

Georgie shares the Easter eggs with Annie and Pippa. How many does each child get?

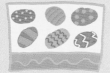

12 ÷ 3 = ?

12 ÷ 3 = 4

You can answer this question with number facts you know (12 ÷ 3 = 4).

Find out more about: multiplication and division as opposites (page 82)

Don't know the starting number

There are 4 packs of batteries in the drawer and 20 batteries altogether. How many batteries are in each pack?

$\boxed{?} \times 4 = 20$ You can answer this question with number facts you know $(5 \times 4 = 20)$.

$\boxed{5} \times 4 = 20$

Or you can use opposites:
The opposite of x4 is ÷4.
20 ÷ 4 = 5, so the missing number is 5.

Oliver has some batteries and 7 toys. He puts 2 batteries in each toy. How many batteries did he have?

$\boxed{?} \div 2 = 7$ You can answer this question with number facts you know $(14 \div 2 = 7)$.

$\boxed{14} \div 2 = 7$

Or you can use opposites:
The opposite of ÷2 is x2.
2 x 7 = 14, so there were 14 batteries.

Don't know what a number was divided or multiplied by

Some children each plant 4 bulbs in a pot. 16 tulips grow. How many children planted the bulbs?

$4 \times \boxed{?} = 16$

You can answer this question with number facts you know $(4 \times 4 = 16)$.

Or you can use opposites: divide the number of tulips by the number of children to find out how many bulbs each child planted.
16 ÷ 4 = 4, so the answer is 4.

There are 30 tulips. Eva used them to make some bunches of flowers. There were 6 tulips in each bunch. How many bunches did she make?

$30 \div \boxed{?} = 6$

$30 \div \boxed{5} = 6$

You can solve the problem with number facts you know $(30 \div 5 = 6)$. Or you can rearrange it and use 30 ÷ 6 = 5.

Checking calculations

It is easy to make mistakes with numbers. (Everyone does it.) It's best to check your calculation by doing it again a different way. Check that the answer makes sense too.

Change the order

You can check multiplication by multiplying the numbers in a different order. The answer should be the same.

To check:

4 x 5 = 20

try:

5 x 4 = 20

The product is the same, so the answer is correct.

Checking doubles

To check doubles, use what you know about halves.

To check:

4 x 2 = 8

try:

8 ÷ 2 = 4

Checking halves

To check halves, use what you know about doubles.

To check:

12 ÷ 2 = 6

try:

6 x 2 = 12

Use opposites

Multiplication and division are opposites, so you can use this to help check your answers.

To check:

18 ÷ 6 = 3

try:

6 x 3 = 18

or:

3 x 6 = 18

This calculation works with the same numbers, so your answer is correct.

To check:

24 ÷ 3 = 8

try:

8 x 3 = 24

This calculation works with the same numbers, so your answer is correct.

Using a calculator

You can use a calculator to multiply or divide numbers, or to check answers. Pages 88 and 89 show you how.

Find out more about: doubles (page 79); halves (page 82); order of multiplication (page 79); products (page 75)

Calculators

A calculator does calculations for you. (Calculations are math questions.) Calculator buttons are called keys. You use them to type in a calculation, then read the answer on the display screen.

Here are the main keys that are on most calculators. On some calculators they are in different places. See if you can find them on your calculator.

C/CE or AC Clear key

This erases the numbers on the display and makes it show 0. Use it before every calculation, or if you make a mistake and want to start again.

Digit keys

Use these keys to put numbers into the calculator.

7	8	9
4	5	6
1	2	3
0	.	

The lowest digits are at the bottom.

Operation keys

+, −, x and ÷ are called operations. These keys add (+), subtract (−), multiply (x) or divide (÷) numbers.

on On key

This key switches the calculator on, so it is ready to use.

Equals key

Press this at the end of a calculation to see the answer.

Constant operation

On some calculators you can also use the equals key to do the last operation again.

Put in a number, press + then press the equals key twice. The calculator will start counting up in groups of that number each time you press =.

Adding in this way is a good way of seeing how repeated addition is like multiplication.

Simple calculations

Use the keys to type in the first number. Press the key of the operation you want. Type in the second number. Press the equals key. The answer will appear on the screen.

To do the calculation 5 × 6, press these keys in this order:

The display will show the answer: 30

Result

Result is another name for the answer.

Calculator games

Using a calculator can help you find out how numbers work. Here are some calculator games you can try.

Making 20
Choose three digits (say, 2, 8, 6). Press + and − and = as often as you like, but only use each digit once. See if you can make all the numbers up to 20.

Five key challenge
See how many ways you can get 20 into the display by pressing just 5 keys. (For example, 15 + 5 = or 10 × 2 =)

Race to zero
Share a calculator. Enter 20 (or 30 or 50). Take turns subtracting a number from 1 to 9. The winner is the person to end up with 0.

Checking calculations

A calculator does just what you tell it to. It is easy to make mistakes, so make sure you put in the numbers that will solve your problem.

Joe has $24 and Mel has $18. How much more money does Joe have than Mel? To solve this problem you need to be able to tell that this is subtraction. You key in

Remember to check your calculations too, by doing them a different way. (See pages 74 and 87.)

Talking about shapes

The shape of something is its outline, or the way it looks from the outside. Here are some useful shape words.

Patterns

A pattern is an arrangement of shapes or lines. Part of a pattern often repeats.

a zigzag pattern   a spotted pattern

Closed shapes

A closed shape has an edge all the way around.

These are closed shapes.

Open shapes

The edges of an open shape do not meet.

These shapes are open.

Flat shapes

A flat shape has no thickness.

These are some flat shapes.

2-D shapes

Flat shapes are also called 2-D shapes. (2-D is short for 2-dimensional.)

Curved

Something that is curved bends.

These lines are curved.

The sides of this bowl are curved.

Straight

Something straight does not bend.

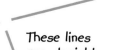

These lines are straight.

The covers of this book are straight.

Round

Something that is round has a shape like a circle or a ball.

This clock face is round.

This orange is round.

Hollow

A hollow shape has empty space inside it.

  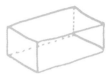

These shapes are hollow.

Solid

A solid shape has no air inside.

These shapes are solid.

Convex

A shape that goes out is convex.

convex shape

Concave

A shape that goes in is concave.

concave shape

Corners

A corner is where two lines, or sides of a shape, meet.

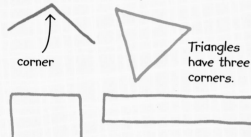

corner

Triangles have three corners.

Squares and rectangles each have four corners.

The size of a corner is an angle. This is the amount you would need to turn one line or side to sit exactly on top of the other one.

There are small angles like this (called acute angles)...

...and bigger angles, like this. (These are called obtuse angles.)

This is a special corner called a right angle. It is a quarter of a whole turn.

Vertex

A vertex is another word for a corner.

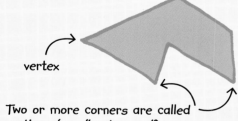

vertex

Two or more corners are called vertices (say "vurty-sees").

Find out more about: quarter turns, right angles, whole turns (page 105)

Sides

The line between two corners of a shape is a side. The side a shape sits on is its base.

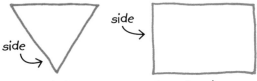

A triangle has three sides.

A rectangle has four sides.

Diagonals

A diagonal is a line which joins two corners that are not next to each other.

The red lines are diagonals.

A diagonal can be outside a shape too.

Regular

All the sides and corners of a regular shape are the same size.

regular hexagon

Irregular

The sides and corners of an irregular shape are not the same size.

irregular hexagon

3-D shapes

3-D shapes have length, width and thickness. (3-D is short for 3-dimensional.) 3-D shapes are often called solids. This can be confusing because hollow shapes are 3-D shapes too.

Surfaces

The surface of something is its outside, or part of its outside.

Faces

A surface of a 3-D shape is called a face. Faces can be flat or curved. The face a shape sits on is its base.

A cube has six flat faces.

A sphere has one curved face.

Edges

The edge of a 3-D shape is the line where two faces meet.

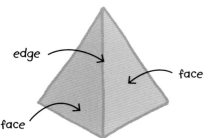

edge

face

face

2-D shapes

2-D shapes are flat. Here are some common 2-D shapes.

Circles

A circle is perfectly round. Something that is shaped like a circle is circular.

Triangles

Any shape with three corners and three straight sides is a triangle. Triangular means shaped like a triangle.

Not all triangles look the same.

Rectangles

A rectangle has four straight sides and all its corners are right angles. Something that is shaped like a rectangle is rectangular.

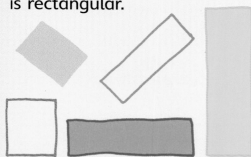

Squares

A square is a special rectangle. Its four sides and four corners are all the same size.

Pentagons

A pentagon has five straight sides and five corners.

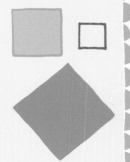

regular pentagon

This pentagon is concave.

Hexagons

A hexagon has six straight sides and six corners.

regular hexagon

This hexagon is concave.

Octagons

An octagon has eight straight sides and eight corners.

regular octagon

This octagon is concave.

Find out more about: concave (page 91); corners (page 91); regular (page 92); right angles (page 91); sides (page 92); straight (page 90)

Sorting shapes

You can put shapes into groups that have something in common. This page shows some groups that you can sort shapes into.

Drawing and making 2-D shapes

You can draw or make shapes that have different numbers of sides. You can use paper marked with dots or grids, or use rubber bands on pegboards.

Shapes with 3 sides

Sometimes you draw shapes by connecting the dots. Here are three different shapes that have three sides. They are all triangles.

Shapes with 4 sides

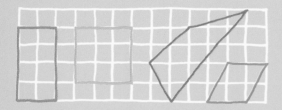

Sometimes you draw shapes on paper with grids printed on them. This is a square grid covered with shapes that have four sides.

Shapes with 5 sides

These shapes all have five sides. They have been drawn on plain paper.

Shapes with 6 sides

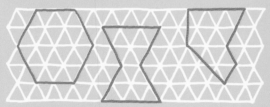

All the shapes drawn on this triangle grid have six sides.

Shapes with right angles

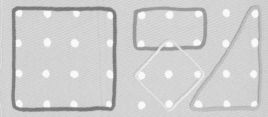

On a pegboard, you can stretch rubber bands around pegs to make shapes. These shapes all have at least one right angle.

Shapes with no right angles

None of the shapes on this pegboard has a right angle in it.

3-D shapes

3-D shapes have thickness. Pictures of 3-D shapes can be difficult to work out, because you are showing a 3-D shape using 2-D shapes.

There are four cubes in this shape.

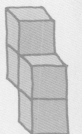

Cubes

A cube has six square faces.

These are cubes.

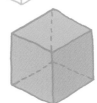

Cuboids

A cuboid has six faces that are all rectangles.

These are cuboids.

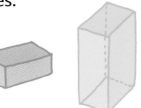

Prisms

A prism has two opposite faces that are the same shape as each other. Its other faces are all rectangles.

These are triangular prisms.

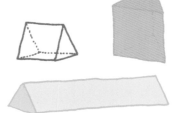

Cylinders

A cylinder has a circle at each end.

These are cylinders.

Pyramids

The sides of a pyramid are triangles. They meet at a point.

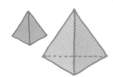
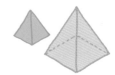

pyramids with a triangular base

pyramids with a square base

Cones

A cone has a curved surface that reaches a point. Its base is a circle.

These are cones.

Spheres

A sphere is perfectly round, like a ball.

These are spheres.

Find out more about: bases (page 92 (faces)); circles (page 93); curved (page 90); faces (page 92); round (page 91); squares, triangles, triangular (page 93)

Making 3-D shapes

You can make 3-D shapes by cutting and folding 2-D shapes drawn on paper or cardboard.

You could fold along the dotted lines on all these flat shapes to make a cube.

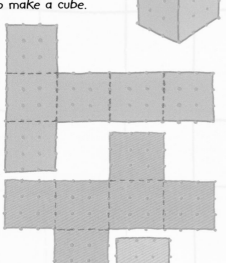

Making words include:

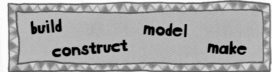

build

construct

model

make

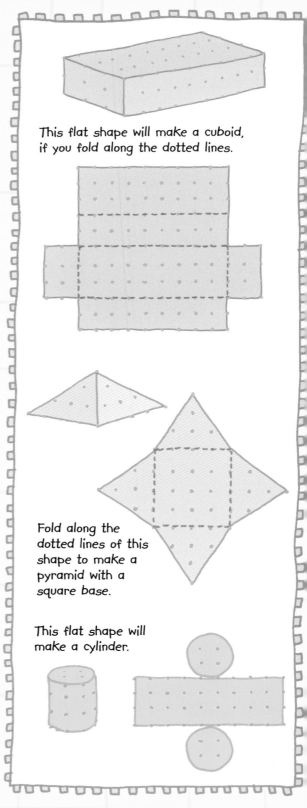

This flat shape will make a cuboid, if you fold along the dotted lines.

Fold along the dotted lines of this shape to make a pyramid with a square base.

This flat shape will make a cylinder.

Line symmetry

In many shapes, one half matches the other like a reflection in a mirror. This is called line symmetry and the shapes are symmetrical.

Symmetrical shapes

This butterfly shape is symmetrical. Each half matches the other.

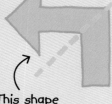

This shape is not symmetrical. Its halves don't match.

To make a symmetrical shape:

1. Fold a piece of paper in half.

2. Draw half a picture along the fold line and cut out your drawing.

3. Unfold the paper to see the shape.

The fold line is its line of symmetry.

Mirror lines

A line that divides a shape in half to give two matching half shapes is called a mirror line.

mirror line

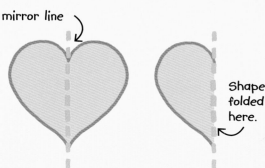

Shape folded here.

When you fold a paper shape along its mirror line, the halves fit together exactly.

Drawing mirror lines

To draw a line of symmetry, draw a straight line that divides the shape into matching halves.

Each half of these shapes is a mirror image. You can put a mirror along the line and see the other half in the mirror.

You can put a mirror along the blue dotted line to complete these shapes.

Find out more about: halves (page 54)

Lines of symmetry

A line of symmetry is another name for a mirror line.

Reflective symmetry

This is another name for line symmetry.

Here are some other useful symmetry words.

match

mirror

reflection

fold

other half

Reflections

You can change a shape by flipping it over. The flipped over shape is called a reflection.

When you look at something in a mirror, or in water, you are looking at a reflection.

object   reflection

The penguin and the dog are looking at their reflections.

object

reflection

A shadow is a reflection too.

Drawing reflections

You can use grids of dots or squares to help you draw a shape's reflection.

1. Choose a corner on the drawing and count how many points there are *between* it and the mirror line.

2. Count the same number of points on the other side of the line and make a mark.

This corner is 4 dots away from the mirror line.

Count 4 dots on the other side of the line and make a mark.

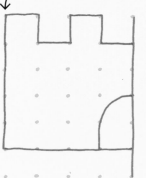

3. Do this for each corner of the drawing, one at a time.

4. When you have finished, connect the dots to see the picture's reflection.

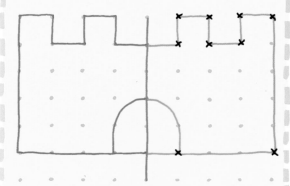

You can use the same method on a square grid, but you count squares instead of dots.

Position

The position of something is its place. There are some position words on pages 45 to 47. Here are some more.

On (on top of)

The purple box is on the red one. You can say it is over it or above it too.

In (inside)

The purple box is inside the red box.

Under

The purple box is under the red one. You can also say it is below, beneath or underneath it.

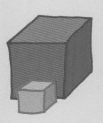

In front / behind

The purple box is in front of the red one. The red box is behind the purple one.

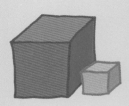

Next to

These boxes are next to, or beside, each other.

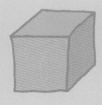

Top

The top of this box is green.

There is a yellow stripe at the top of this card.

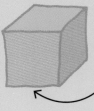

Bottom

The bottom of the box is underneath it, so you can't see it here.

The stripe at the bottom of this card is green.

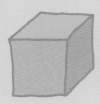

Side

The sides of this box are purple.

The stripes at the sides of this card are purple.

Outside
The outside of this box has yellow spots on it.

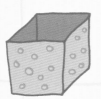

Inside
The inside of the box is plain purple.

Front
The front of the box below is blue.

You can't see the back on this picture.

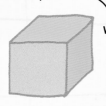

Back
The back is the part farthest from the front.

Middle (center)
This square has a circle in the middle. Center means middle too.

Edge
This square has purple stripes around the edges.

Opposite
Opposite means facing. The opposite sides and corners of this square are shown in the same colors.

The blue sides and corners are opposite. The reds are opposite too.

Close
Things that have a short way between them are close. Another word for close is near.

These boats are close together.

Apart
Apart means away from something else.

These boats are apart.

Far
Things that have a long way between them are far.

These boats are far apart.

Between
Something that is between has things on both sides of it.

The red boat is sailing between the two red buoys.

Similar meanings

The words in each box have similar meanings to each other.

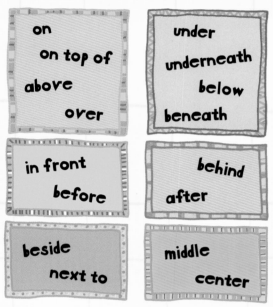

on
on top of
above
over

under
underneath
below
beneath

in front
before

behind
after

beside
next to

middle
center

Opposite meanings

The words in each pair below have opposite meanings.

over	under
above	below
top	bottom
in front	behind
front	back
before	after
middle	edge
together	apart
outside	inside
on	in

Coordinates

You can use letters and numbers to give the position of something on a grid or map. These letters and numbers are coordinates.

Each square on the grid has a letter (shown at the bottom of the grid) and a number (shown at the side of the grid). Here is a map of a desert island.

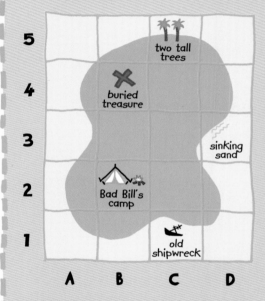

The two tall trees are at C5. The sinking sand is at D3. Bad Bill's camp is at B2. The old shipwreck is at C1.

To find the coordinate of the treasure, look at the letter of the square it is in (B) and the square's number (4). The coordinate of the buried treasure is B4.

101

Movement

When something moves, it changes position, from one place to another. Changing place is called movement.

Journey

The path something takes to get from one place to another is its journey.

Route

Route is another word that means journey.

Direction

Direction is the way something goes to get to a place. Here are some useful direction words:

Up

When something moves up, it goes from a lower place to a higher place.

 On paper up is shown as an arrow like this.

 This rocket is zooming up.

Down

When something moves down, it goes from a higher place to a lower place.

 On paper down is shown as an arrow like this.

 This parachute is drifting down.

Left

When something moves left, it goes toward the direction of your left hand.

left hand

 On paper an arrow like this shows left.

 This car is facing left.

Right

When something moves right, it goes toward the direction of your right hand.

right hand

 This car is facing right.

 On paper an arrow like this shows right.

Higher
Higher means closer to the top.

The purple kite is higher than the orange kite.

The purple kite is lower than the blue kite.

Lower
Lower means closer to the bottom.

Forward
Moving forward means moving toward the front.

These trucks are going forward.

You count forward along a number line this way.

0   1   2   3   4   5   6

Backward
Moving backward means moving toward the back.

These trucks are going backward.

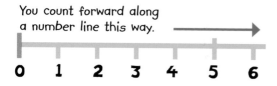

0   1   2   3   4   5   6

You count backward along a number line this way.

Sideways
Moving sideways means moving toward one side or another. Things can move sideways to the left or right.

This crab moves sideways.

Across
Moving across means moving from one side of something to the other.

This cloud is moving across the sun.

Along
Moving along means moving on or next to a line or path.

This train is moving along the track.

Through
Moving through something means moving inside it from one side to the other.

The dolphin is leaping through the hoop.

Find out more about: back (page 100); bottom (page 99); front (page 100); inside (page 100); left (page 102); next to (page 99); on (page 99); right (page 102); side (page 99); top (page 99)

Toward (to)

Moving toward something means moving in the direction of it, so it is getting closer.

This cat is moving toward the mouse.

Away from (from)

Moving away from something is moving in the opposite direction of it, so it is getting farther.

The mouse is running away from the cat.

Around

Moving around something is moving outside it in a circle.

The bee is flying around the flower.

Slide

When you slide a shape you move it to another place without turning or flipping it over.

To move the yellow K to the position of the purple K, you must slide it along and down (or down and along).

Turning

Turning a shape means moving it around in a circle. Another word for turning is rotation.

Scissor blades turn around a point.

A greeting card opens around a line.

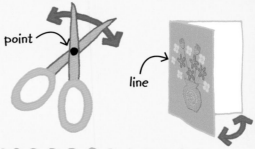

point

line

Clockwise

Moving clockwise means moving in a circle around to the right, like the hands on a clock.

These arrows show which way is clockwise.

Counterclockwise

Moving counterclockwise means moving in a circle around to the left.

These arrows are pointing counterclockwise.

To take the lid off a jar you turn it counter-clockwise.

Whole turns

A whole turn is a complete turn all the way around.

a whole turn

Half turns

A half turn is a half of a whole turn.

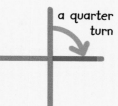
a half turn

Quarter turns

A quarter turn is a quarter of a whole turn.

a quarter turn

This is what happens when you turn a K in quarter turns clockwise around its middle.

Right angles

A right angle is another name for a quarter turn.

This symbol means the corner is a right angle.

Roll

When something rolls it moves by turning over and over.

You might roll a ball or dice.

Compass points

You can use compass points to describe direction or to give the position of places.

These are the four main compass directions.

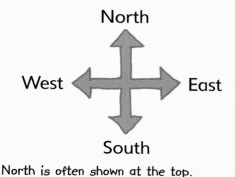

North is often shown at the top.

Stretch

Stretching something makes it bigger in one direction.

Stretching a circle makes an oval.

Bend

Bending something changes its shape so it is not straight.

You can bend a flat sheet of paper into a cylinder.

Find out more about: clockwise (page 104); corners (page 91); cylinders (page 93); direction (page 102); position (page 99)

Size and measuring

The size of something is how big it is or how much of it there is. You can find out something's size by measuring it.

Measuring something will tell you how big it is, and weighing it will tell you how heavy it is. Its age is a measure of how old it is.

Estimating size

Estimating the size of something means taking a good guess. Estimating before you measure something can help you know if your measurement makes sense.

Here are some other words that mean estimate.

predict
approximate
guess

Comparing

When you compare things you look at them carefully to see if they are the same or different. You can compare all kinds of things, such as how tall, or heavy or old they are.

When you compare these plants you can see several things about how tall they are.

C is shortest.

A
B
C
D

A is tallest.

B and D are the same height.

Ordering

When you have compared things, you can put them in order. This means you give each thing a place because of how big, heavy, old (or whatever) it is.

These plants are in order of height from smallest to biggest.

Very berry smoothie
You will need:
  2 cups of apple juice
  3 cups of strawberries
  2 scoops of ice cream
  1 banana (chopped)
  2 tall glasses
  2 paper umbrellas

Too little

If there is too little of something there is less than you need.

Mel has cut up too little banana.

Too many

If there are too many of something there are more than you need.

Mel has too many umbrellas.

Enough

If you have enough of something you have as much as you need.

Mel has enough juice for the recipe.

Too few

If there are too few of something there are not as many as you need.

There are too few glasses.

Not enough

If there is not enough of something there is less than you need.

There are not enough strawberries for the recipe.

Just over

If a size is just over an amount, it is a little more than it.

There is just over half a glass of smoothie.

Too much

If there is too much of something there is more than you need.

Mel has put out too much ice cream.

Just under

If a size is just under an amount, it is a little less than it.

There is just under half a glass of smoothie.

About

About means close to.

These carrots are about the same length.

Here are some other words that mean about.

> nearly   close to
>
> almost
>
> to the nearest
>
> just over   roughly
>
> approximately
>
> about the same as
>
> just under

Exactly

Exactly means not more than and not less than.

These pencils are exactly the same length.

Accurate

An accurate measurement is exactly correct.

When to measure

Sometimes estimating or comparing tells you as much as you want to know.

Lou's train is longer than Jed's.

Lou's train

Jed's train

Sometimes you want to know more, and measuring tells you the size more exactly.

Lou's train is 2 cars longer than Jed's.

Units

A unit is a fixed amount of something. You use different units to measure different things.

Inches and feet are units of length.

Ounces and pounds are units of weight.

Minutes and hours are units of time.

Non-standard units

Non-standard units are objects that are the same size as each other but that not everyone uses for measuring. Here are some non-standard units.

This bracelet is 8 paperclips long.

These bananas weigh 72 marbles.

It takes 180 hippopotamuses to boil an egg. (You say "one hippopotamus, two hippopotamus...")

Standard units

Standard units are units that everyone in a country uses for measuring. Here are some standard units.

1 yard

5 pounds

5 pounds   1 quart

Measurement

A measurement is a number and a unit that tells you about the size of something.

The measurements of this page are about $6\frac{3}{4}$ inches across, and $9\frac{1}{2}$ inches from top to bottom.

Measuring scales

A measuring scale is a set of lines and numbers that you can use to find a measurement. The lines are called markers or divisions, and they stand for units. A measuring scale is often just called a scale.

The scale on this ruler shows units called inches. Each marker shows 1 inch.

marker

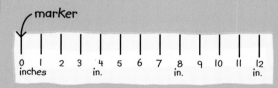

0 1 2 3 4 5 6 7 8 9 10 11 12
inches   in.   in.   in.

The scale on this measuring cup shows units called fluid ounces. Each marker stands for 2 fluid ounces.

The scale on this kitchen scale is in a circle. This scale shows units called pounds. Each marker stands for a half pound.

Find out more about: fluid ounces (page 119); inches (page 114); pounds (page 116); quarts (page 119); yards (page 114)

Length

Length is how far it is from one end of something to the other.

Measuring the length of this truck will tell you how long it is.

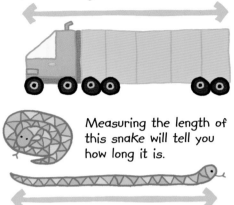

Measuring the length of this snake will tell you how long it is.

Length can also be the distance from one end of a room to the other.

Long

Something long has a big length. Long is the opposite of short.

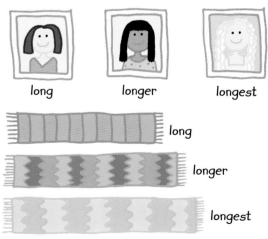

long   longer   longest

long

longer

longest

When you measure how long something is, you find out how far it is from end to end.

Height

Height is how far it is from the bottom of something to its top. It is also how far above the ground an object is.

The height of this helicopter is how far it is off the ground.

The height of this house is measured from bottom to top.

Your height is the measurement from your feet to the top of your head.

High

Something high is a long way from the ground. High is the opposite of low.

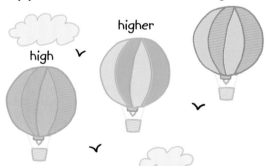

high

higher

highest

Tall

Something tall is a long way from its bottom to its top. Tall is the opposite of short.

tall   taller   tallest

Width

Width is how far it is across something from side to side.

The width of this picture frame is its measurement from side to side.

The width of a river is its measurement from side to side.

When you measure how wide something is, you find out how far it is from one side to the other.

Wide

Something wide measures a lot from side to side. Wide is the opposite of narrow.

wide house   narrow house

Narrow

Something narrow has a small measurement from side to side. Narrow is the opposite of wide.

Depth

Depth is how far something is from top to bottom. Depth sometimes means how far it is from front to back too.

The depth of a fish tank is its measurement from top to bottom.

The depth of a shelf is its measurement from front to back.

When you measure how deep something is, you find out how far down (or far back) it goes.

Deep

Something deep measures a lot from top to bottom (or from front to back). It is the opposite of shallow.

deep bowl

shallow bowl

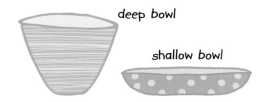

Shallow

Something shallow has a small measurement from top to bottom (or from front to back). It is the opposite of deep.

Find out more about: measurement (page 109)

Big

Something big takes up a lot of space. Something bigger takes up more space and the biggest things takes up the most space. Big is the opposite of small.

These words mean big, bigger and biggest too:

great
greater
greatest

large
larger
largest

Big, great and large are very general words, so it is better to use a word that really means what you want to say. She is taller than me, this chair is wider than that one, and so on.

Small

Something small is little. Small, smaller and smallest are opposites of big, bigger and biggest.

Low

Something low is close to the ground. Low is the opposite of high.

low   lower   lowest

Short

Something short has a small length. Short is the opposite of tall and long.

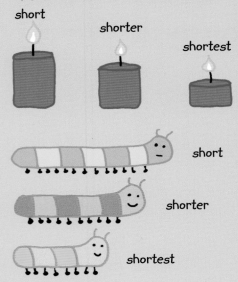

short
shorter
shortest

short
shorter
shortest

Thick

Something thick is deep or wide. It is the opposite of thin.

thick sandwich   thin sandwich

THICK   THIN

thick letters   thin letters

Thin

Something thin is narrow or shallow. It is the opposite of thick.

Distance

Distance is the amount of space between two points.

The distance from the start to the finish is the amount of space between them.

Near

Something near is a short way away. It is the opposite of far.

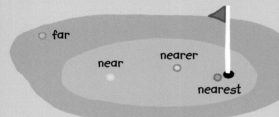

These words mean near, nearer and nearest too:

close   closer   closest

Far

Something far is a long way away. Far is the opposite of near.

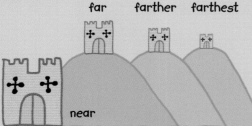

Non-standard units

Here are some useful non-standard units you can use to measure length.

Pencils

To measure small things using pencils, or other small objects, lay them along the thing you want to measure.

This strip of ribbon is 2 pencils long.

Hands

A handspan is the distance between your thumb and little finger, when you stretch out your hand.

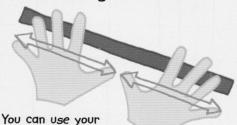

You can use your hands to measure things such as tables and chairs.

Steps or paces

A step or pace is the distance between your feet when you walk.

Use steps or strides (long steps) for measuring longer distances, such as the length of a room.

Find out more about: length (page 110)

Standard units of length

Standard units for measuring length, height, width and depth are inches, feet and yards.

Inches (in.)

An inch is a unit of distance. You use inches to measure short lengths. You will see inches on many rulers and tape measures. "in." is short for inches.

This line is exactly 1 inch long.

This square is 1 inch tall and 1 inch wide.

12 inches = 1 foot

Feet (ft.)

A foot is a unit of distance. You use feet to measure longer lengths. You will see feet on rulers, tape measures and yard sticks. "ft." is short for feet.

3 feet = 1 yard

Yards (yds.)

Yards are units of distance for lengths that are longer than three feet. You will find yards on yard sticks and tape measures. "yds." is short for yards.

Rulers

A ruler has inches marked on it. You use it for measuring short lengths and to help you draw straight lines.

Most rulers are 12 inches but there are shorter and longer ones too.

Yard sticks

A yard stick is like a long ruler. It is 1 yard (or 3 feet) long. You use it for measuring longer lengths, such as people, tables or chairs.

A yard stick is 36 inches long.

Tape measures

A tape measure is flexible. You can use it for measuring around things, such as your waist or a tree trunk. Some tape measures are very long.

You might use a tape measure to measure curved objects such as this prize-winning pumpkin.

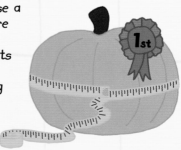

Reading scales

Rulers, yard sticks and tape measures have measuring scales on them. When you measure something, you find its length by reading the scale.

Always look carefully at the scale to make sure you know what the markers show.

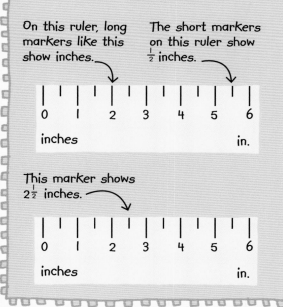

On this ruler, long markers like this show inches.

The short markers on this ruler show $\frac{1}{2}$ inches.

This marker shows $2\frac{1}{2}$ inches.

The metric system

In other parts of the world people use a different system of measurement called the metric system. This uses centimeters and meters to measure lengths and distances.

Measuring lines

To measure a line with a ruler:

1. Place the ruler along the line, with the 0 marker at one end of it.

2. Look at the scale and see which marker is closest to the other end of the line. This is the measurement.

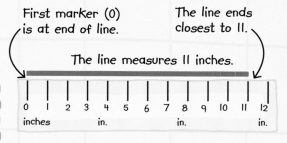

First marker (0) is at end of line.

The line ends closest to 11.

The line measures 11 inches.

Drawing lines

To draw a line that is, say, 7 inches long:

1. Draw a dot where you want the line to start.

2. Put a ruler on the page, with the marker that means 0 under the dot.

3. Find the marker that shows 7 inches (or another length you want) and draw another dot above it.

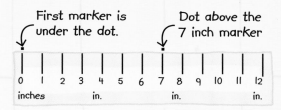

First marker is under the dot.

Dot above the 7 inch marker

4. Use your pencil and ruler to draw a straight line connecting the dots. The line will be the length you measured.

Find out more about: measuring scales (page 109)

Mass and weight

Mass is the amount of stuff something is made of. Its weight is how heavy it is.

Weigh

When you weigh something you find out how heavy it is.

Balance

When two things balance on weighing scales they weigh the same as each other and do not tip the scales either way.

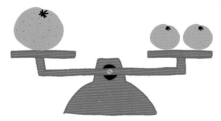

These scales balance, so the big orange weighs the same as the two little ones.

Heavy

Something heavy weighs a lot.

heavy   heavier   heaviest

Light

Something light weighs a little.

lightest

lighter

light

When you put things in order of weight, the size is not important. A brick is heavier than a cardboard box. A pebble is heavier than a balloon.

Ounces (oz.)

An ounce is a unit of weight. You use ounces to measure small weights. You will find ounces on scales. "oz." is short for ounces.

16 ounces = 1 pound

2,000 pounds = 1 ton

Pounds (lbs.)

You use units called pounds to measure big weights. You will find pounds on bathroom scales, and things like bags of flour. "lbs." is short for pounds.

Tons

The heaviest weights are measured using tons.

Weighing scales

You use weighing scales to find out how heavy something is. Here are some different types.

Balancing scales

Put the thing you are weighing on one side, and add weights to the other side until the scales balance. Add the measurements written on the weights to find the weight of the object.

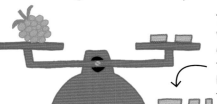

These are weights. You use them to find out how heavy things are.

Kitchen scales

When you put objects in the bowl, the finger moves around the dial to show the weight.

Electronic scales show the weight digitally, like this.

8 oz.

Spring balances

A spring balance has a hook on the bottom, where you hang the thing you're weighing.

The marker is pulled down the scale and shows the weight.

Reading a scale

Kitchen scales have a measuring scale on them. You read the scale to find its weight. Always look at the scale to make sure you know what the markers show.

To read a scale, look where the finger is pointing and see which marker it is closest to.

The arrow is pointing to 1, so the pineapple weighs 1 pound.

The arrow is pointing to halfway between 0 and 1 pound, so the melon weighs half a pound, which is 8 ounces.

The metric system

In some parts of the world the metric system is used to measure how heavy things are. Metric units for weighing things include grams and kilograms.

Find out more about: markers, measuring scales (page 109)

Capacity

Capacity is the amount of space inside something.

This bucket has a big capacity.

This cup has a small capacity.

Holds

To hold means to have room for something. For example, a cup holds a small amount and a bathtub holds a large amount.

Contains

An object that contains something has that thing inside it.

This cup contains juice.

Container

A container is anything that can hold something inside it.

Boxes, bottles and pitchers are containers.

Some

Some means an amount of something.

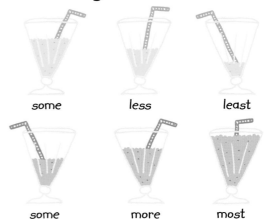

some   less   least

some   more   most

Full

Something that is full has no empty space inside it.

full

Empty

Something empty has nothing in it.

empty

Half full

Something half full contains the same amount of stuff and empty space.

Jamie poured some juice into his cup and now it is half full.

half-full

Half empty looks the same as half full, but it usually means it was more full to start with.

Nia drank some juice and now her cup is half empty.

Fluid ounces (fl. oz.)

People measure small amounts in fluid ounces. You find ounces on measuring cups. "oz." or "fl. oz." is short for fluid ounces.

32 fluid ounces = 1 quart

Quarts (qt.)

A quart is a unit of capacity. You find quarts on measuring cups. "qt." is short for quarts.

4 quarts = 1 gallon

Half a quart is called a pint. "pt." is short for pints.

1 pint = 16 fluid ounces

Gallons (gal.)

A gallon is a unit of capacity used to measure big amounts, such as the amount of water in a swimming pool. "gal." is short for gallons.

The metric system

In some parts of the world the metric system is used to measure volume. Metric units of capacity include liters and milliliters.

Measuring containers

There are different kinds of measuring containers you can use to find out how much space is filled by something.

Use measuring cups to measure larger amounts.

You use teaspoons, tablespoons and measuring cups to measure when cooking.

Reading a scale

Measuring containers often have a measuring scale on them. You read the scale to find out how full they are, or to measure out the right amount of liquid to use in a recipe.

To read a scale, look where the top of the liquid is and see which marker it is closest to.

The top of the water is closest to the 24 fl. oz. marker, so there are 24 fl. oz. water in this cup.

Find out more about: measuring scales (page 109)

Time

Time is how long something takes to happen, or the interval between two events.

The time

The time is a particular moment, shown on a clock or watch.

Days

A day starts and ends at 12 o'clock at night. There are 24 hours in a day.

Weeks

A week is seven days long.

Weekends

A weekend is Saturday and Sunday.

Months

A month is about 4 weeks long. The days in each month are numbered in order starting at 1.

Years

A year is 12 months long. Years are numbered in order, for example 2012, 2013, 2014.

Days of the week

Sunday
Monday
Tuesday
Wednesday
Thursday
Friday
Saturday

Months of the year

January	31 days
February	28 (or 29) days
March	31 days
April	30 days
May	31 days
June	30 days
July	31 days
August	31 days
September	30 days
October	31 days
November	30 days
December	31 days

This rhyme will help you remember how many days the months have.

Thirty days has September,
April, June and November;
All the rest have thirty-one,
Excepting February alone,
Which has twenty-eight days clear,
And twenty-nine in each leap year.

Useful time words

Calendars A calendar is a list of all the days, weeks and months in a year.

Dates A date is the number of a day and the month it is in. For example May 7th.

Birthdays Your birthday is the date you were born.

Holidays A holiday is a day when you do not have to go to school or to work. People often spend some holidays away from home.

Seasons A season is part of the year. Many areas of the world have four seasons: spring, summer, fall and winter. Some places have fewer seasons, such as a rainy season and a dry season.

Day Day is the time when it is light outside.

Night Night is the time when it is dark outside.

Noon Noon is 12 o'clock in the middle of the day.

Midnight Midnight is 12 o'clock in the middle of the night.

am "am" tells you what time of day it is. "am" starts at midnight and ends just before noon. 6:00 am is 6 o'clock in the morning.

pm "pm" tells you what time of day it is. "pm" starts at noon and ends just before midnight. 9:00 pm is 9 o'clock at night.

Morning Morning is the daytime before noon.

Afternoon Afternoon is the daytime from noon until about 6 o'clock pm.

Evening Evening is between about 6:00 pm and 9:00 pm.

Today Today is the day that is happening now.

Tomorrow Tomorrow is the day after today.

Yesterday Yesterday is the day before today.

Before   Something that happens before something else happens earlier in time. May is before June.

After   Something that happens after something else happens later. Tuesday is after Monday.

First   When something happens first, nothing happens before it.

Next   When something happens next, it follows straight on from something else. The next day after Monday is Tuesday.

Last   When something happens last, nothing happens after it.

Now   Now means at this time.

Soon   Soon is in a short time.

Early   Early means near the beginning of something. Early in the day means in the morning. Earlier is more early.

Speed of time How quickly time seems to go depends on how interested you are in what you are doing. Time passes slowly when you are bored, and quickly when you're having fun.

Late   Late means near the end of something. Late in the day means in the evening. Later means more late.

Quick   Something quick takes a short time to happen. Something quicker takes less time, and the quickest thing takes the shortest time.

Fast   Something that is fast can move quickly.

fast   faster   fastest

Slow   Something slow takes a long time to go somewhere or to do something.

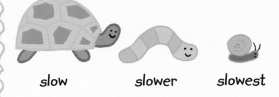

slow   slower   slowest

Old   Something old has existed for a long time. Older means more old. The oldest thing has existed for the longest time.

New   Something new has just been made. Newer means more new. The newest thing was made the least time ago.

How often?

The question "how often?" asks how many times. Here are some answers.

Always Always means every time or all the time.

The sun always rises.

Usually When something usually happens, it happens almost every time.

Kim usually brushes her teeth twice a day.

Often Something that happens often happens a lot.

Dark clouds often bring rain.

Sometimes Something that happens sometimes happens at some times but not at others.

Twice Something that happens twice, happens two times.

Once Something that happens once, happens only one time.

"Once upon a time..."

You have a birthday once a year.

Never Something that never happens does not happen at all.

How long?

"How long?" asks how much time. A long time is a lot of time and a short time is a little.

How long is there between 9:15 and 10:30?

How long ago? This asks how much time was it before now that something happened.

How long ago were you born?

How long will it take to? This asks how much time does something need to happen.

"How long will it take to get there?"

How long will it be until? This asks how much time is it from now until something happens in the future.

How long will it be until Christmas?

Takes longer Something that takes longer needs more time for it to happen.

It takes longer to put shoes on than to take them off.

Takes less time Something that takes less time needs a shorter time for it to happen.

Telling the time

You measure the time of day in hours and minutes. Very short moments are measured in seconds. When you tell the time, you look at a watch or clock and read the time it shows.

1 day = 24 hours

1 hour = 60 minutes

1 minute = 60 seconds

Digital clocks

Digital clocks shows the time in numbers, separated by two dots.

The first number is the hour.

The number after the dots tells you how many minutes.

To tell the time, say what you see. This clock is showing eleven fifteen, which is 15 minutes past 11.

Analog clocks

An analog clock has a face with numbers 1 to 12 on it. A short pointer, called the hour hand, shows which hour it is. A long pointer, called the minute hand, shows the minutes. The hands move clockwise.

It takes 5 minutes for the minute hand to move from one number to the next. It takes 1 hour for the hour hand to move between numbers.

...O'clock
When the long hand is on the 12, the time is "... o'clock."

4 o'clock (4:00)

Quarter past ...
When the long hand is on the 3, the time is "quarter past ..."

quarter past 4 (4:15)

Half past ...
When the long hand is on the 6, the time is "half past ..."

At half past 4 (4:30) the hour hand is halfway between 4 an 5.

Quarter to ...
When the long hand is on the 9, the time is "quarter to ..."

quarter to 5 (4:45)

In 3 hours and 15 minutes, the hour hand will have moved on 3 hours from 5 to 8. The minute hand will have moved on 15 minutes to the o'clock position.

8 o'clock (8:00)

Money

Money is the name for the coins and bills you use to buy things. Coins are made of metal and bills are made of paper.

Different countries have different coins and bills.

Currency

Different countries often have different kinds of money. The money a country uses is called its currency.

US currency is called dollars. It uses dollars and cents. There are 100 cents in 1 dollar.

> **$ is the sign for dollars.**
> **¢ or c stands for cents.**
> **$1 = 100¢**

Other countries use different currencies. For example, the UK currency is called pounds sterling and uses pence and pounds.

> **£ is the sign for pounds.**
> **p is short for pence.**
> **£1 = 100p**

Value

Value is how much something is worth. Coins and bills have different values. The US has coins worth 1¢, 5¢, 10¢ and 25¢. Less common are 2¢, 50¢ and $1 coins.

Buy

When you buy something, you give money so you can have it. When you have bought something, you have given money for it.

Sell

Selling something means giving it to someone for money. If you have sold something, someone has given you money for it.

Spend

When you spend money, you use it to buy things. When you have spent money, you have used it to buy things.

Pay

Paying means giving money to buy something.

Sale! Everything must go!

$6 $3 $18 $15 $4 $12

Price and cost

The price of something is the amount of money you need to buy it. How much something costs is its price.

You can say that the price of the ball is $4 or that the ball costs $4.

Total cost

To find the total cost, add together the prices of all the things you want to buy.

The total cost of the ball, the car and the penguin is $13. ($4 + $6 + $3)

Change

Change is the money you are given back when you pay too much for something. To find how much change you need, subtract the cost from the money you are paying.

How many cars can Sam buy for $15? How much change will he have?

1 car costs $6.
2 cars cost $12.
(3 cars cost $18 so $15 is not enough to buy three.)
$15 - $12 = $3.
Sam will have $3 change.

$6

Costs more

Something that costs more has a higher price.

Pricey

Something pricey is expensive. It has a high price and costs a lot.

Costs less

Something that costs less has a lower price.

Cheap

Something cheap has a low price and does not cost much.

$12 $15 $18

$6 $4 $3

pricey   pricier   priciest   cheap   cheaper   cheapest

All about data

In math, information is called data. There are lots of ways to collect data, sort it, and show it to other people.

Counting

A simple way to collect information is to count it.

Vote

When you vote for something you choose it. Collecting votes is a good way to find out what people like, such as which food, band or sport they like best.

Data lists

A data list shows each piece of information as you get it. Data like this needs to be sorted so it's easier to see what it shows.

Ice cream choices

C C V S S
S C C C V
C C V S C
S S C V S

20 children voted for the ice cream they liked best. This data list shows their votes.

C stands for chocolate

V stands for vanilla

S stands for strawberry

Tally charts

Making marks called tallies can help you keep track of data that you count. (You can find out how to make tallies on page 13.) A tally chart is a list with tallies against each thing you are counting.

Ice cream choices

Chocolate   卌 IIII

Strawberry   卌 II

Vanilla   IIII

These tallies show the ice cream choices of 20 people.

You can see that chocolate has the most votes and vanilla has the fewest.

Tables

A table is a list that shows data in rows and columns. It makes data easier to read.

This table shows how many of 20 people liked each kind of ice cream best.

Ice cream choices	
Ice cream	Number of people
Chocolate	9
Strawberry	7
Vanilla	4

Find out more about: columns (page 32); counting (pages 12-23); rows (page 32)

Sorting

When you sort things you look at them and put them into groups, or sets, of things that are alike in some way.

Sorting diagrams

Sorting diagrams show how things are related to each other. Tree diagrams, Carroll diagrams and Venn diagrams are kinds of sorting diagrams.

Tree diagrams

A tree diagram helps you sort things by answering questions with only two possible answers.

These numbers have been sorted using a tree diagram.

14　45　19
36　31
22　8　1

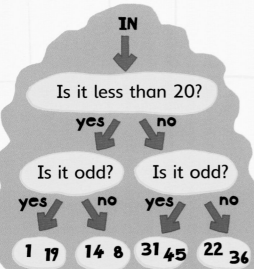

Venn diagrams

A Venn diagram uses circles to sort things into groups called sets.

These fruits have been sorted into groups using a Venn diagram.

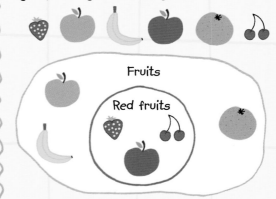

Like all sorting diagrams, you can use Venn diagrams to group things in different ways.

These numbers can be sorted in different ways using a Venn diagram.

1 2 3 4 5 6 7 8 9 10
11 12 13 14 15 16 17 18 19 20

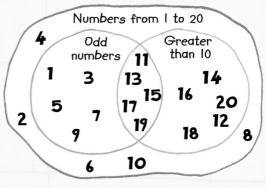

The diagram above helps you find odd numbers greater than ten, but you could use similar diagrams to sort numbers into different groups, such as even numbers and multiples of 3.

Carroll diagrams

A Carroll diagram lets you sort things into groups using a grid.

These shapes have been sorted into two groups using a Carroll diagram.

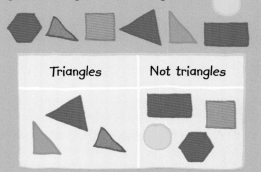

Here, the same shapes have been sorted into four groups using a Carroll diagram.

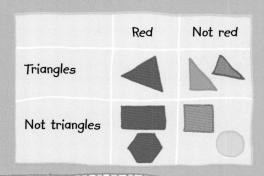

Showing information

Charts or graphs show data. When you have collected and sorted data, you can draw a chart or graph to show the data to other people. Pictograms, block graphs and bar charts are types of charts you can draw.

Titles

A title tells people what data a graph or chart is showing. For example "Trips to school."

Labels

A label tells you what something is. Labels on graphs and charts help people to understand the data.

Represents

Represents means stands for.

Popular

Something popular is liked by many people. The most popular thing is liked by the highest number of people. The least popular thing is liked by the fewest people.

Common

When something is common you see lots of them. The most common thing is the thing you see the greatest number of. The least common thing is the thing you see the smallest number of.

Find out more about: bar charts (page 131); block graphs (page 130); data (page 127); groups (page 52); pictograms (page 130)

Pictograms

A pictogram uses pictures to show data. Each picture stands for an amount.

Fruits we like best

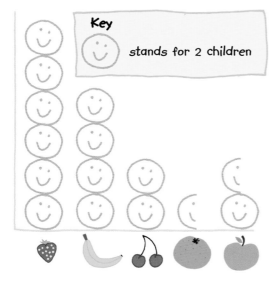

Key

😊 stands for 2 children

To find out how many children liked each fruit best, count the faces above each fruit and multiply the number by 2.

Pictograms can tell you lots of information quickly. Here are some things this pictogram shows.

Strawberries were most popular with this group of children.

Oranges were least popular.

The fruits that are liked best by 3 children are apples.

12 children liked strawberries best.

There are 4 more children who like bananas best than who like cherries best.

Axes

↶The lines at the bottom and side of a chart or graph are called axes (say "ak-sees"). Each line is called an axis. ↘

Block graphs

A block graph uses blocks to show data. Each block stands for an amount.

Transportation to school

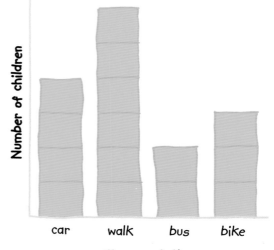

Count the blocks for each type of transportation to find out how many children come to school each way. Here are some of the things this graph shows.

6 children walk to school.

3 children bike to school.

Twice as many children go to school by car as by bus.

Bar charts

A bar chart uses thick lines called bars to show data. Numbers and labels on the axes help to show what the bars represent.

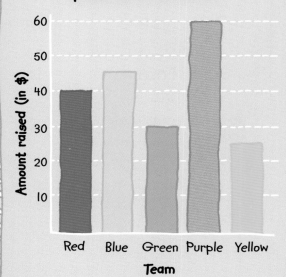

Sponsored run totals

To find out how much money a team raised in their sponsored run, find the top of the team's bar and look at the numbers on the side axis to see the amount.

Here are some of the things this bar chart shows.

The purple team raised the most money. They raised $60.

The yellow team raised the least. Their bar is halfway between the $20 and $30 markers, so they raised $25.

The team that raised $30 is the green team.

The total raised by all the teams is $200.

Hila collected some data by counting the number of letters in the names of her friends. She kept a tally of the number of names with 3 letters, 4 letters and so on. Then she counted the tallies and drew a bar chart to show her data.

This is Hila's tally chart and bar chart.

Number of letters	Tally	Total
3	IIII	4
4	IIII	5
5	IIII IIII II	12
6	IIII III	8
7 or more	III	3

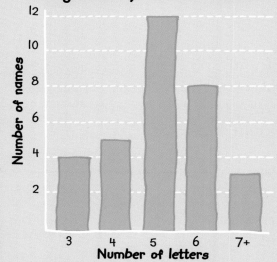

Length of my friends' names

Here are some of the things Hila's bar chart shows.

The most common name length is 5 letters.

4 more of her friends have 6-letter names than 3-letter names.

More of Hila's friends have names with 3 letters than with 7 or more letters.

Word finder

Acknowledgements

Web researcher: Sarah Khan
American editor: Carrie Armstrong
US math consultant: Sabrina Ripp

Numicon © Oxford University Press. Numicon is published by Oxford University Press.
www.numicon.com and Numicon materials are reproduced with their permission.